MAYER SMITH

A Legacy in Disguise

First edition

Contents

One

A Stranger in Town

The late afternoon sun hung low in the sky, casting an amber glow over the quiet town of Willow Creek. Dust swirled in the dry air as the stranger strolled into view, his silhouette framed by the hazy light. He walked with the deliberate ease of someone used to being overlooked. A battered hat shadowed his face, and his coat, frayed at the edges, seemed to have seen better days. No one paid him much attention, except for a few children playing near the fountain who whispered and giggled before being shooed away by their mothers.

The stranger stopped at the general store, the faded wooden sign creaking as it swung in the light breeze. He pushed the door open, and a small bell jingled, announcing his arrival. The storekeeper, a rotund man with thinning hair and a perpetual scowl, looked up from his ledger.

"Help you with something?" the storekeeper grunted.

"A room," the stranger replied, his voice calm and measured. "And some work, if you've got any leads."

The storekeeper squinted at him, clearly suspicious. "New in town?"

The stranger nodded, his expression unreadable. "Just passing through."

The storekeeper grunted again but scribbled something on a scrap of paper. "Try Mrs. Miller's boarding house, two blocks down. She's always looking for a hand to fix things up. But she don't take kindly to trouble."

"No trouble from me," the stranger assured, tipping his hat slightly before leaving the store.

Out on the street, the townsfolk cast furtive glances his way. Some muttered to each other, while others avoided eye contact entirely. It wasn't often that someone new came to Willow Creek, and when they did, they were usually gone before long.

As the stranger walked, he noted the peeling paint on the buildings, the cracked cobblestones of the main street, and the sagging porches of homes that once might have been grand. The town wore its age like a tired traveler, every creak and crack a testament to its faded glory.

At the corner of the street, he paused. A woman stood with

her back to him, struggling to balance a large basket of laundry while opening the door to what appeared to be a small sewing shop. Her auburn hair caught the sunlight, shimmering like fire. She muttered a curse under her breath as the basket tilted precariously.

"Need a hand?" the stranger offered, stepping closer.

Startled, the woman turned, her green eyes locking onto his. She hesitated for a moment, clearly assessing whether he was a threat. Then she gave a curt nod.

"Fine. Just don't drop it," she said, stepping aside to let him take the basket.

The stranger lifted it effortlessly, his strength belying his lean frame. He followed her inside, where the scent of lavender and aged wood filled the air. The shop was small but tidy, with bolts of fabric neatly stacked on shelves and a sewing machine sitting prominently on the counter.

"Set it there," she instructed, pointing to a table by the window. "Thanks."

He placed the basket down and turned to leave, but her voice stopped him.

"You're not from around here, are you?"

He glanced back at her, his expression guarded. "No."

"Figured as much. People don't just stroll into Willow Creek without a reason. What are you looking for?"

"Work," he replied simply. "And a place to stay."

She raised an eyebrow, folding her arms. "Mrs. Miller's, then?"

He nodded.

"She'll take you in if you're willing to put up with her rules. And if you're staying long enough to pay your way."

"I'll manage," he said, tipping his hat again before stepping out into the street.

The woman watched him go, her curiosity piqued. There was something about the way he carried himself—calm, confident, but with an air of mystery that made her uneasy. She shook her head, dismissing the thought. Willow Creek didn't need any more secrets.

—-

That evening, the stranger found himself seated at a rickety table in Mrs. Miller's cramped kitchen. The boarding house was as worn as the rest of the town, its walls covered in faded wallpaper and its floors creaking with every step. Mrs. Miller, a stern woman in her sixties, served him a bowl of stew without a word, her sharp eyes scrutinizing him as if she could uncover his past with a single glance.

"You'll earn your keep," she said finally. "Fix the roof, chop the firewood, and keep to yourself. I don't tolerate gossip or trouble under my roof."

"Understood," he replied, his tone respectful but firm.

As the night wore on, the stranger sat by the small window in his room, staring out at the darkened streets. The distant sound of a train whistle echoed through the night, a haunting reminder of the world beyond Willow Creek. He reached into his pocket and pulled out a weathered photograph, its edges frayed and its image faded. In it, a younger version of himself stood beside a grand estate, his arm draped protectively over the shoulders of a woman whose face was obscured by time.

His jaw tightened as he tucked the photo away. This town was just a stop on his journey, a place to lay low until he could figure out his next move. But something about Willow Creek felt different—like the calm before a storm.

—-

Meanwhile, across town, the auburn-haired woman stood in her sewing shop, staring out the window into the inky blackness. Her thoughts drifted back to the stranger, his steady gaze and quiet demeanor lingering in her mind. There was a weight to him, a gravity that she couldn't explain.

Her thoughts were interrupted by a sharp knock at the door. She turned, startled, as the door creaked open to reveal a figure cloaked in shadow.

"Who's there?" she demanded, her voice steady despite the unease creeping over her.

The figure stepped forward, revealing a familiar face twisted in anger. "You need to stay away from him," the man growled. "He's trouble."

Her heart raced, but she stood her ground. "I don't know what you're talking about."

"Yes, you do," the man spat. "He's not who he says he is. And if you get involved, you'll regret it."

Before she could respond, the man turned and disappeared into the night, leaving her with more questions than answers.

As the stranger lay in bed that night, listening to the creaks and groans of the old house, he felt the weight of his secret pressing down on him. He had come to Willow Creek to escape the ghosts of his past, but it seemed they had followed him here. And in this quiet town, where everyone had something to hide, the line between friend and foe was already beginning to blur.

Two

Secrets in the Dark

The moon was a pale sliver in the night sky, casting an eerie glow over Willow Creek. The streets were quiet, save for the occasional rustle of leaves carried by the wind. Inside Mrs. Miller's boarding house, the stranger lay awake, staring at the cracked ceiling of his room. Sleep eluded him, as it often did these days. His mind churned with thoughts of the past he had left behind and the uncertain future that lay ahead.

A soft creak outside his door snapped him from his thoughts. He sat up, listening intently. The floorboards groaned under the weight of someone moving cautiously down the hallway. He slipped out of bed, his movements practiced and silent, and pressed his ear to the door. The sound of footsteps grew fainter, heading toward the back of the house.

Curiosity tugged at him. He had learned to trust his instincts, and tonight they whispered of something amiss. Pulling on his boots and jacket, he eased the door open, careful not to make a sound. The hallway was dimly lit by the faint glow of moonlight streaming through the window at the far end. The footsteps had stopped, but he caught the faint sound of a door clicking shut.

The back door.

The stranger moved swiftly but cautiously, his footsteps soundless on the wooden floor. He reached the back door and slipped outside into the cool night air. The yard behind the boarding house was overgrown, the grass tall and untamed. He scanned the shadows, his sharp eyes adjusting quickly to the darkness.

Then he saw it—a figure moving near the edge of the property, heading toward the woods. Whoever it was, they were moving with purpose, their steps quick and deliberate. Without hesitation, the stranger followed, keeping to the shadows and staying downwind.

The woods were dense, the trees standing like silent sentinels. The sound of rustling leaves and the occasional hoot of an owl filled the air. The stranger kept his distance, his movements careful and deliberate. The figure ahead of him carried a lantern, the faint glow bobbing through the darkness like a will-o'-the-wisp.

As they ventured deeper into the woods, the stranger began to notice signs of disturbance—a broken branch here, a scuffed patch of earth there. Someone had been through this path before, and recently. His pulse quickened as he wondered what could bring someone out here in the dead of night.

The figure ahead came to a stop in a small clearing. The stranger crouched behind a tree, his breathing steady as he observed. The lantern was set on the ground, casting flickering shadows across the scene. The figure—a man, by the looks of his build— knelt beside a patch of disturbed earth and began digging with his hands.

The stranger's brow furrowed. What could the man be looking for? Gold? A hidden stash? Or perhaps something darker?

The man pulled something from the ground, a small metal box caked with dirt. He wiped it clean with the sleeve of his coat and opened it. The stranger couldn't see the contents from where he crouched, but he could tell by the man's reaction that it was significant. The man froze for a moment, then quickly closed the box and tucked it into his coat.

Suddenly, the man stood and turned sharply, his eyes scanning the woods. The stranger pressed himself against the tree, holding his breath. The man's gaze lingered on the spot where the stranger was hidden, and for a moment, it seemed as though he might have been spotted.

But then the man turned away, picked up his lantern, and started back toward the boarding house, his pace quicker than before. The stranger waited, his muscles tense, until the man was well out of sight. Then he crept forward, his boots barely making a sound on the forest floor.

He approached the spot where the man had been digging and knelt down. The earth was loose, the hole shallow. He ran his fingers through the soil, searching for any clue as to what had been buried there. His fingers brushed against something hard, and he pulled it free—a small, broken piece of metal that looked like it had been part of the box.

Turning it over in his hands, he saw faint markings etched into the surface. They were too worn to make out in the dim light, but something about them felt familiar. He tucked the piece into his pocket and stood, his mind racing. Whatever had been in that box, it was important enough for someone to risk sneaking out in the dead of night to retrieve it. And now, he had a piece of the puzzle.

—-

Back at the boarding house, the stranger slipped inside and headed for his room. He was careful to avoid the creaky spots on the floor, his ears straining for any sign of movement. The house was quiet, the only sound the faint ticking of a clock in the sitting room.

He closed the door to his room and locked it, his heart still pounding from the adrenaline. Sitting on the edge of his bed, he pulled the metal fragment from his pocket and examined it under the faint light of the oil lamp on the nightstand. The markings were clearer now—symbols, perhaps, or letters in a script he didn't recognize. He traced them with his finger, his mind trying to make sense of their meaning.

A soft knock at his door startled him. He slipped the metal piece into his jacket and stood, his hand instinctively reaching for the knife he kept hidden in his boot.

"Who is it?" he asked, his voice low.

"It's me," came a soft voice from the other side of the door. The auburn-haired woman from the sewing shop.

He hesitated for a moment, then unlocked the door. She stood in the hallway, her green eyes wary but determined.

"We need to talk," she said, stepping inside before he could protest. She closed the door behind her and crossed her arms. "I saw you following him."

He raised an eyebrow, surprised. "You were out there?"

She nodded. "I had a feeling something was going on, so I followed him too. And I saw you, trailing behind like some shadow."

He leaned against the wall, his expression unreadable. "And what do you want?"

"To know what you're hiding," she said, her gaze steady. "You're not just some drifter passing through town. You're here for a reason."

The stranger didn't respond immediately. He studied her, weighing his options. Finally, he spoke, his voice measured. "You don't know what you're getting yourself into."

"Maybe not," she admitted. "But I know enough to see that whatever's happening here is bigger than you or me."

Their eyes locked, the air between them tense with unspoken truths. For the first time, the stranger felt the walls he had built around himself begin to crack. But he couldn't let them fall—not yet.

"Go home," he said finally, his voice soft but firm. "This isn't your fight."

She opened her mouth to argue but thought better of it. With a reluctant nod, she turned and left, leaving the stranger alone with his thoughts.

As the door clicked shut, he let out a heavy sigh. The secrets of Willow Creek were beginning to unravel, and he had a sinking feeling that his own secrets would soon follow.

Three

Whispers of Betrayal

The morning dawned cold and gray, with the sky choked by clouds that promised rain. The stranger stood by the window of his room, his hands clasped behind his back as he watched the street below. The town was waking slowly, the few early risers shuffling about their business with the sluggishness of a Monday morning. He spotted Mrs. Miller sweeping the front porch, her broom scratching against the wooden planks, her sharp eyes scanning the quiet street.

Something felt off. It wasn't the kind of unease that came from lack of sleep or lingering guilt—it was something deeper, a weight pressing against his chest, warning him that trouble was brewing.

The fragment of metal from the night before sat on the small wooden table beside him, its edges catching the pale light.

He had spent hours staring at the strange markings, trying to decipher their meaning, but they remained stubbornly inscrutable. Now, they felt like a taunt, a puzzle with no solution.

A sharp knock at the door startled him. He turned quickly, his body tensing.

"Who is it?" he called, his voice steady.

"It's Mrs. Miller," came the brusque reply. "You've got a visitor."

The stranger frowned. A visitor? He hadn't been in town long enough to know anyone well, and he'd taken pains to avoid drawing attention to himself. Crossing the room, he opened the door to find Mrs. Miller standing there with her ever-present scowl.

"Someone downstairs asking for you," she said, her tone clipped. "Says he's an old friend."

His frown deepened. "What's his name?"

"Didn't give one. Says he'll only speak to you."

The stranger nodded. "I'll be right down."

Mrs. Miller turned on her heel and disappeared down the hall. The stranger grabbed his coat, slipping the metal fragment into his pocket, and headed downstairs. The creak of the old wooden steps echoed in the quiet house, each sound amplifying the tension building in his chest.

When he reached the sitting room, a tall man stood with his back to the door, gazing at the collection of faded photographs on the mantelpiece. He wore a dark coat, impeccably tailored, and a hat that obscured his face. Even without seeing him, the stranger knew who it was.

"Marcus," the stranger said, his voice flat.

The man turned slowly, a cold smile curling his lips. His eyes were sharp, calculating, and held a glint of mockery. "You've been hard to find, old friend."

"I wasn't hiding," the stranger replied, stepping into the room. "Just keeping to myself."

"Is that what you call this little charade?" Marcus gestured broadly, his tone dripping with disdain. "You, playing the humble drifter, skulking about in the shadows. It's almost laughable."

The stranger's jaw tightened, but he didn't rise to the bait. "What do you want?"

Marcus chuckled, the sound low and mirthless. "Straight to the point, as always. I've come to deliver a message. A warning, really."

The stranger folded his arms, his expression unreadable. "I'm listening."

Marcus stepped closer, his voice dropping to a conspiratorial whisper. "You're walking a dangerous line, my friend. Sticking your nose where it doesn't belong. There are people who won't take kindly to your… curiosity."

The stranger met his gaze, unflinching. "Is that a threat?"

"It's advice," Marcus said smoothly. "You've always had a knack for getting yourself into trouble. But this time, you might not make it out."

The room was thick with tension, the air heavy with the weight of unspoken history. The stranger knew better than to trust Marcus. They had once been allies of convenience, but those days were long gone, and their paths had diverged in ways that could never be reconciled.

"I'll keep that in mind," the stranger said finally, his tone dismissive.

Marcus's smile faltered, his eyes narrowing. "Be careful, my friend. The past has a way of catching up to you."

With that, he turned and strode out of the room, his footsteps echoing on the wooden floor. The stranger watched him go, his mind racing. Marcus's presence in Willow Creek wasn't a coincidence. He was here for a reason, and whatever it was, it spelled trouble.

—-

That evening, the stranger sat alone in the small diner on Main Street, nursing a cup of black coffee. The place was nearly empty, the quiet hum of the radio providing a soft backdrop to the clatter of dishes in the kitchen. The waitress, a cheerful young woman with freckles and a quick smile, had stopped by his table once to refill his cup but hadn't lingered.

He was grateful for the solitude. He needed time to think, to piece together the fragments of the puzzle that seemed to grow more convoluted with each passing day. The metal fragment, Marcus's cryptic warning, the man in the woods—they were all connected, but how?

As he stared into his coffee, a familiar voice broke through his thoughts.

"You've been busy."

He looked up to see the auburn-haired woman from the sewing shop standing by his table. Her green eyes sparkled with a mix of curiosity and defiance, and her hands were planted firmly on her hips.

"Mind if I sit?" she asked, not waiting for an answer before sliding into the seat across from him.

He raised an eyebrow but didn't protest. "You're persistent."

"I could say the same about you," she shot back. "What's your game, stranger? You come into town, act all mysterious, and then start poking around where you don't belong. People are talking."

He leaned back in his seat, studying her. "And what are they saying?"

She shrugged. "That you're trouble. That you've got secrets."

He smirked, though it didn't reach his eyes. "Everyone's got secrets."

"True," she admitted. "But not everyone has someone like Marcus paying them a visit."

His expression darkened. "You were eavesdropping."

"Hard not to, when the whole house echoes like that." She leaned forward, lowering her voice. "Who is he? And what does he want from you?"

The stranger hesitated. He had no reason to trust her, but something about her tenacity was oddly compelling. Still, he couldn't afford to let her get too close.

"Stay out of it," he said finally, his tone firm. "This doesn't concern you."

Her eyes narrowed, and for a moment, he thought she might argue. But then she leaned back, crossing her arms. "Fine. Keep your secrets. But don't think for a second that I'm going to sit by and let you bring trouble to this town."

With that, she stood and walked away, her shoulders squared and her head held high. The stranger watched her go, a pang of regret tugging at him. He didn't want to involve her—or anyone else—but it seemed fate had other plans.

As the door to the diner swung shut behind her, the stranger pulled the metal fragment from his pocket and turned it over in his hands. The symbols etched into its surface seemed to mock him, their meaning just out of reach. He knew he was running out of time. Whatever secrets Willow Creek held, they were closing in on him fast. And if he wasn't careful, they would consume him whole.

Four

Shadows Beneath the Surface

The storm struck just before dusk, rolling in from the horizon with an unsettling ferocity. Thick clouds churned across the sky, blotting out the last rays of sunlight. Rain lashed the streets of Willow Creek, turning the dusty roads into a slick, muddy mess. The wind howled through the cracks in the boarding house, rattling the windows as if it were trying to claw its way inside.

The stranger stood in his room, the weak light of a single oil lamp illuminating his stoic face. He stared at the metal fragment in his hand, the etched symbols now fully visible under the faint glow. They still made no sense, yet they felt ominously familiar, like a word on the tip of his tongue that refused to come to him. He turned it over again, hoping for a revelation that didn't come.

A loud knock broke through the storm's din, echoing from downstairs. His head snapped up, his instincts kicking in. He tucked the fragment into his coat pocket and moved swiftly to the door, opening it just wide enough to glance down the hall. Nothing. But the knock came again, louder this time, as though whoever was outside was growing impatient.

He descended the stairs silently, each step a calculated move. When he reached the bottom, Mrs. Miller was already standing in the foyer, a candle clutched in her hand. Her face was pale, her usually stern expression replaced by one of nervous curiosity.

"Who could be out in this weather?" she muttered, glancing back at him as he joined her.

"Stay back," he said, his voice low but commanding. He approached the door cautiously, the howling wind outside masking any sounds of movement. With one hand, he slid the bolt free and eased the door open.

A figure stood on the porch, drenched from head to toe. It was the auburn-haired woman from the sewing shop, her clothes plastered to her skin and her eyes wide with alarm. She stepped forward, clutching something tightly to her chest—a leather-bound book that was nearly as soaked as she was.

"Let her in," Mrs. Miller said sharply, breaking the tension. The stranger stepped aside, and the woman stumbled in, water pooling around her feet as the storm raged behind her.

"What are you doing here?" the stranger asked, his tone sharper than he intended.

"I didn't know where else to go," she said, her voice trembling. She held up the book, her hands shaking. "This belonged to my father. I found it hidden in the attic… and I think it's connected to you."

His eyes narrowed, his gaze dropping to the book. The leather cover was worn and cracked, its edges frayed with age. A broken clasp dangled from one side, and faint, faded writing was barely legible on the front.

"What's in it?" he asked.

"I don't know," she admitted. "The pages are… strange. Some of it's written in a language I can't read, and the rest doesn't make sense. But look at this."

She flipped open the book, revealing a page with a drawing that made the stranger's blood run cold. It was a sketch of a sigil, intricate and hauntingly familiar, almost identical to the markings on the metal fragment in his pocket.

"Where did you find this?" he demanded, his voice low.

"I told you, in the attic," she said, her green eyes flashing with a mix of fear and defiance. "It was hidden under the floorboards."

Mrs. Miller, who had been watching silently, cleared her throat. "This feels like a conversation that shouldn't happen in my hallway," she said pointedly. "Take it to the sitting room."

The stranger nodded, gesturing for the woman to follow him. They moved into the dimly lit room, the storm outside casting flickering shadows on the walls. He closed the door behind them and turned to face her.

"Why did you bring this to me?" he asked.

"Because you're connected to it somehow," she said. "I don't know how, but I can feel it. And I think my father was too."

"Your father," he echoed, his tone unreadable. "What happened to him?"

She hesitated, her hands tightening around the book. "He disappeared when I was a child. One day, he went into the woods and never came back."

The stranger's jaw tightened. This town was steeped in secrets, and it seemed her family had its share of them too.

He reached into his pocket and pulled out the metal fragment, holding it up for her to see. Her eyes widened as she stepped closer, her gaze darting between the fragment and the book.

"They match," she whispered.

"Exactly," he said. "Whatever this is, it's bigger than you or me."

She opened the book again, flipping through the pages until she found another drawing. This one showed a map, its edges faded but its lines still distinct. A symbol, the same sigil from before, was marked in the corner, alongside coordinates written in a script neither of them could decipher.

"This map," she said, tracing her finger along its lines. "I think it leads somewhere in the woods."

The stranger leaned over her shoulder, studying the map. It was crude but detailed enough to be useful. He recognized the general layout of the area—an old logging trail, the winding river, and a clearing marked with an 'X.'

"You're not thinking of going out there," she said, her voice tinged with worry.

"I don't have a choice," he replied. "This isn't just a coincidence. If your father was involved in whatever this is, it's tied to my past too."

"And you're just going to walk into the woods in the middle of a storm?" she asked incredulously. "Alone?"

He met her gaze, his expression hard. "I've been alone for a long time. I know how to handle myself."

Her lips pressed into a thin line, but she didn't argue further. Instead, she placed the book on the table and stepped back. "Then you'd better take this."

The stranger hesitated, then nodded. He tucked the book under his arm and turned toward the door.

"Be careful," she said softly.

He paused, glancing back at her. For a moment, he considered telling her to leave, to go back to her shop and forget about all of this. But he knew it was too late for that. She was already entangled in the web, just as he was.

Without another word, he slipped out into the storm, the book held tightly against his chest. The rain pounded against him, soaking him to the bone as he made his way toward the woods. The wind whipped through the trees, their branches clawing at the sky like desperate hands.

With every step, the sense of foreboding grew stronger. Whatever lay ahead, he knew it would change everything.

Five

The Forbidden Path

The woods were alive with the storm, the wind howling through the trees like a wounded animal. Rain poured relentlessly, soaking the stranger as he trudged deeper into the forest. The map clutched in his hand was quickly deteriorating under the onslaught of rain, its fragile paper threatening to dissolve into nothing. He had memorized the key landmarks earlier, committing the faint lines and crude drawings to memory, but doubt gnawed at him. What if he had misunderstood? What if this path led to nowhere?

The sound of his boots squelching in the mud was muffled by the cacophony of the storm. Each step felt heavier than the last as he pushed through the underbrush, the weight of the leather-bound book tucked under his arm a constant reminder of the mystery he was unraveling. The symbols etched in his mind—the sigil, the cryptic markings on the metal fragment—seemed to hum with an energy he couldn't explain.

The forest grew darker as the storm thickened. Shadows stretched and danced in the dim light, twisting into shapes that played tricks on his mind. He reached the remnants of an old logging trail, its once-cleared path now overgrown with weeds and brambles. According to the map, this trail would lead him to the clearing marked with the 'X.'

He paused, glancing over his shoulder. The sensation of being watched was a familiar one, but tonight it felt particularly sharp. The hair on the back of his neck prickled, and his instincts screamed that he wasn't alone. He tightened his grip on the book and continued forward, his every sense on high alert.

The path wound deeper into the forest, the trees closing in around him like a fortress. Lightning cracked across the sky, illuminating the woods for a brief moment. In that flash of light, he thought he saw movement—a shadow darting between the trees, too quick and deliberate to be the wind. He stopped, his breath catching in his throat.

"Who's there?" he called, his voice steady despite the storm's fury.

No response. Only the wind, the rain, and the rustling of leaves.

He stood still, scanning the trees for any sign of movement. His hand drifted to the knife hidden in his boot, a precaution he had carried for years. After a tense moment, he began walking again, slower this time, his eyes constantly darting to the shadows.

The trail ended abruptly at a steep incline, the ground slick with mud. Above him, the clearing loomed, shrouded in mist and darkness. He climbed carefully, digging his boots into the earth for traction. The rain made the ascent treacherous, and twice he slipped, catching himself on the exposed roots of nearby trees.

When he reached the top, the clearing stretched out before him, eerily silent. The storm seemed to falter here, the wind dying down to a whisper and the rain softening to a drizzle. In the center of the clearing stood an ancient stone altar, its surface worn smooth by time and weather. The sigil from the book and the fragment was carved into its face, glowing faintly as if reacting to his presence.

The stranger approached cautiously, every instinct screaming at him to turn back. The air around the altar felt charged, humming with an energy that made his skin crawl. He placed the book on the altar, its soaked cover seeming to dry instantly as it touched the stone.

A sudden rustling behind him made him whirl around, knife in hand. His heart raced as the auburn-haired woman stepped into the clearing, her face pale but determined.

"What are you doing here?" he demanded, his voice low and sharp.

"I followed you," she said, stepping closer. "You weren't going to tell me anything, so I had to see for myself."

"You shouldn't be here," he snapped. "It's dangerous."

"Do you even know what you're dealing with?" she countered, her voice rising. "That altar, those symbols—they're connected to something bigger than you or me. My father—"

Her words were cut off by a low growl, the sound vibrating through the air. The stranger froze, his eyes darting to the treeline. A pair of glowing eyes stared back at him, unblinking and predatory. The creature stepped into the clearing, its massive form partially obscured by the mist. It was unlike anything he had ever seen—part wolf, part shadow, its body seeming to shift and blur as though it were made of smoke.

"Get behind me," he said, his voice a harsh whisper. The woman hesitated for only a moment before doing as he said.

The creature moved slowly, its movements deliberate and almost mocking. It sniffed the air, its glowing eyes locked on the altar. The stranger tightened his grip on the knife, though he knew it would be useless against whatever this was.

As the creature approached, the sigil on the altar began to glow brighter, pulsing in time with the stranger's racing heartbeat. The book trembled, its pages flipping wildly as though caught in an invisible wind. A deep, guttural voice filled the clearing, speaking in a language neither of them understood.

The creature stopped, its gaze shifting between the stranger and the woman. It let out a bone-chilling howl, and the ground beneath them began to tremble. The stranger grabbed the woman's arm and pulled her back, positioning himself between her and the creature.

"What do we do?" she whispered, her voice trembling.

"Stay behind me," he said. "And if I tell you to run, you run. Don't look back."

The creature lunged, faster than the stranger anticipated. He barely had time to react, raising the knife in a desperate attempt to defend himself. The blade sliced through the creature's smoky form, but it had no effect. The creature swiped at him with claws made of shadow, knocking him to the ground.

The woman screamed, but she didn't run. Instead, she grabbed the book from the altar and held it up, its pages glowing with a blinding light. The creature recoiled, its form flickering as though it were struggling to hold itself together.

"Keep going!" the stranger shouted, scrambling to his feet.

She flipped through the book, her hands shaking as she searched for something—anything—that could help. The sigil on the altar pulsed brighter, and the creature let out another howl, this one filled with rage and pain.

Finally, she found a page marked with the sigil and began to read the words aloud. Her voice was shaky at first but grew stronger as she continued. The air in the clearing seemed to shift, the charged energy focusing on the creature.

The stranger watched in awe as the creature writhed, its form breaking apart under the power of her words. With a final, ear-splitting howl, it dissolved into nothing, leaving the clearing silent once more.

The woman collapsed to her knees, the book slipping from her hands. The stranger rushed to her side, his heart pounding.

"Are you okay?" he asked, his voice hoarse.

She nodded weakly. "What… what was that?"

"I don't know," he admitted, his gaze drifting to the altar. "But whatever it was, it's not over."

The sigil continued to glow faintly, a haunting reminder of the power that had been unleashed. The stranger knew they had only scratched the surface of the mysteries hidden in Willow Creek, and the deeper they dug, the more dangerous it would become.

Six

A Web of Lies

The storm's aftermath left Willow Creek cloaked in a strange, oppressive stillness. The morning sun struggled to pierce through the heavy fog that clung to the trees, casting long shadows over the town. In the boarding house, the stranger sat at the small wooden table in his room, staring at the leather-bound book. Its once waterlogged pages were now crisp and dry, as if the storm had never touched them.

The symbols within taunted him, their meaning still elusive. He traced the sigil on the cover with his finger, feeling the faint grooves under his touch. The memory of the creature in the clearing haunted him, its glowing eyes and smoky form etched into his mind. It wasn't just a warning; it was a promise of more to come.

A knock at the door startled him from his thoughts. He closed the book quickly, shoving it under the loose floorboard where the metal fragment already lay hidden.

"Come in," he said, his voice steady.

The door creaked open, revealing Mrs. Miller. She stepped inside, her sharp eyes narrowing as they swept over him. In her hands, she held an envelope.

"This came for you," she said, her tone unreadable. She set it on the table and lingered for a moment. "Strange, though. Nobody saw who delivered it."

The stranger nodded, waiting for her to leave. She hesitated but finally turned and left the room, the sound of her footsteps fading down the hall.

He picked up the envelope, noting the absence of a return address. His name wasn't written on it—only a single word, scrawled in an unfamiliar hand: Beware.

His pulse quickened as he tore it open. Inside was a single sheet of paper, folded neatly. He unfolded it and read the message written in bold, black ink:

"Trust no one. Even those closest to you."

He stared at the words, his mind racing. It could be a warning— or a trap. Either way, it meant someone was watching him, someone who knew more than they should. The sense of isolation he had always relied on to keep himself safe felt suddenly fragile, as though it could be shattered at any moment.

—-

Later that day, he ventured into town, the letter tucked securely in his pocket. The streets were quiet, the usual hum of activity muted. It was as if the storm had unsettled everyone, leaving a lingering unease in its wake.

The sewing shop was empty when he arrived, the bell above the door jingling faintly. He stepped inside, his gaze sweeping over the neatly organized shelves of fabric and the sewing machine sitting idle on the counter. The woman wasn't here.

He turned to leave but paused when he noticed a piece of paper pinned to the back of the counter. It was a list, handwritten in the same neat script he recognized from the book. The items on it were mundane—thread, buttons, fabric swatches—but at the bottom was a single word that made his blood run cold: Altar.

The door creaked open behind him, and he turned sharply to see the woman step inside. She froze when she saw him, her expression shifting from surprise to something more guarded.

"What are you doing here?" she asked, her tone sharp.

"I could ask you the same thing," he replied, his gaze dropping briefly to the list. "Care to explain this?"

She followed his gaze and her eyes widened. For a moment, she seemed genuinely shocked, but then her expression hardened. "That's just a list of supplies. It's nothing."

"Nothing?" he echoed, his voice rising. "The altar is nothing? After what we saw last night?"

She opened her mouth to respond, but no words came. Instead, she turned away, busying herself with rearranging a stack of fabric. Her hands trembled slightly.

"You're hiding something," he said, his voice low and accusatory. "And I'm not leaving until you tell me what it is."

She slammed her hands on the counter, spinning to face him. "You think you're the only one with secrets?" she snapped. "My father disappeared because of this! Whatever this… this thing is, it destroyed my family. Do you think I want to be part of it?"

"Then why are you?" he pressed, stepping closer.

"Because I don't have a choice!" she shouted, her voice cracking. "Because if I don't figure this out, it'll destroy me too!"

Her words hung in the air, the weight of them suffocating. For the first time, he saw the fear in her eyes, the vulnerability she had been trying so hard to hide. It softened his resolve, but only slightly.

"You don't trust me," he said quietly.

"How can I?" she shot back. "You won't even tell me who you

really are."

The silence that followed was deafening. He didn't have an answer, not one she would believe. The truth was a tangle of lies, and he wasn't sure he could untangle it without breaking everything.

"I don't trust easily," he admitted finally. "But if we're going to survive this, we have to work together."

She studied him for a long moment, her expression unreadable. Finally, she nodded. "Fine. But no more secrets."

He wanted to agree, but the weight of the letter in his pocket reminded him that secrets were sometimes the only thing keeping him alive.

—-

That night, he returned to the boarding house with more questions than answers. He sat at the small table in his room, the book and the fragment laid out before him. The symbols seemed to shift in the flickering light of the oil lamp, as though taunting him with their hidden meaning.

He pulled the letter from his pocket and read it again. "Trust no one. Even those closest to you." The words echoed in his mind, their warning impossible to ignore.

A soft creak outside his door made him freeze. He slipped the fragment into his pocket and closed the book, his hand drifting to the knife hidden in his boot. The creak came again, followed by the faint sound of footsteps.

He moved silently to the door, pressing his ear against it. The footsteps paused, then continued down the hall. He waited, his muscles tense, until the sound faded into silence.

When he finally opened the door, the hallway was empty. But on the floor, just outside his room, lay a small, folded note. He picked it up, his heart pounding, and unfolded it.

"The web tightens. Watch your back."

The handwriting was the same as the letter he had received earlier. His pulse quickened as he realized what it meant. Someone wasn't just watching him—they were inside the boarding house.

He locked the door and leaned against it, his mind racing. The web of lies around him was tightening, and he couldn't shake the feeling that he was being drawn into something far darker than he had ever imagined. The storm outside had passed, but within him, a new storm was brewing—a storm of doubt, fear, and the unshakable sense that the walls were closing in.

Seven

The Shadowed Manor

The moon hung low in the sky, casting an otherworldly glow over the dilapidated manor on the outskirts of Willow Creek. Its once-grand silhouette now stood as a ghostly reminder of a forgotten past, the structure crumbling under the weight of time and neglect. Ivy crept along its weathered stone walls, weaving through shattered windows and climbing toward the gabled roof. The air around the manor was thick, oppressive, as though the very ground it rested on resented its presence.

The stranger stood at the edge of the overgrown lawn, hidden by the shadows of a cluster of oak trees. He had followed the map from the book, each turn leading him closer to this decaying monument. The manor wasn't marked explicitly on the map, but its location aligned with the coordinates near the sigil. If there were answers to be found, they would be inside.

He adjusted the hood of his coat, the chill of the night creeping into his bones. The silence was deafening, broken only by the occasional rustle of leaves in the wind. A single lantern hung near the manor's entrance, its weak light flickering against the night. Someone was here—or had been recently.

He crept forward, his footsteps muffled by the soft carpet of moss and fallen leaves. The manor loomed larger as he approached, its darkened windows like hollow eyes watching his every move. The wooden door was ajar, a sliver of dim light spilling out onto the cracked stone steps. He paused, listening intently for any sign of movement. Nothing.

Pushing the door open further, he stepped inside. The air was damp and stale, heavy with the scent of mildew and decay. The foyer stretched before him, its marble floors covered in a fine layer of dust. A grand staircase wound upward into darkness, its banister splintered and warped. Faded tapestries clung to the walls, their once-vibrant colors reduced to muted shades of gray and brown.

He moved cautiously, his hand brushing against the hilt of his knife. The weight of the metal fragment in his pocket was a constant reminder of why he was here. Every creak of the floorboards beneath his boots sent a jolt of tension through his body.

The flickering light he had seen from outside came from a lantern resting on a table in the center of the room. Next to it was a scattering of papers, their edges curling with age. He approached the table, his eyes scanning the room for any signs of a trap. The papers appeared to be letters, written in the same cryptic language as the book.

He picked one up, studying the symbols. They seemed almost alive, shifting and twisting under his gaze. A chill ran down his spine, and he set the letter back on the table. Whatever this language was, it wasn't meant for human understanding.

A sound broke the silence—a faint shuffle coming from deeper within the manor. He froze, his hand gripping the hilt of his knife. The sound came again, closer this time. Someone—or something—was moving.

He extinguished the lantern on the table, plunging the room into darkness. His eyes adjusted quickly, the faint moonlight filtering through the broken windows providing just enough illumination to navigate. He moved silently toward the source of the noise, his every sense heightened.

The sound led him down a narrow hallway, the walls lined with peeling wallpaper and portraits whose faces had been scratched out. The air grew colder with each step, and a low hum seemed to vibrate through the floor. At the end of the hallway, a door stood slightly ajar, a faint glow emanating from within.

He pushed the door open slowly, revealing a room that seemed untouched by time. The furniture was ornate and well-preserved, the fireplace crackling with a warm, inviting fire. A figure sat in a high-backed chair near the hearth, their face obscured by shadows.

"You've come," the figure said, their voice low and smooth. It was a man's voice, familiar yet distant, like an echo from a half-forgotten memory.

The stranger stepped inside, his grip tightening on the knife at his side. "Who are you?"

The man leaned forward, revealing a face partially obscured by a dark hood. His eyes gleamed with a predatory intelligence, and a faint smile played on his lips. "A guardian. A keeper of secrets. And perhaps… an ally, if you're willing."

"I don't need allies," the stranger replied, his voice cold. "I need answers."

The man chuckled softly. "Then you've come to the right place. But answers come at a price."

"What price?" the stranger demanded, his patience wearing thin.

The man gestured to a small table beside him. On it rested another book, smaller and less worn than the one the stranger carried. Its cover bore the same sigil, glowing faintly in the firelight.

"Take this," the man said. "It will guide you to what you seek."

The stranger hesitated, his instincts screaming that this was too easy. "Why are you helping me?"

The man's smile widened. "Because your fate is tied to mine. And because you're running out of time."

Before the stranger could respond, the fire in the hearth flared violently, filling the room with an intense heat. The man stood abruptly, his figure towering and imposing. "Go now, before it's too late."

The stranger grabbed the book and backed toward the door. The fire roared louder, consuming the room in a blinding light. He turned and ran, the hallway stretching endlessly before him. The hum in the floor grew louder, almost deafening, as the manor seemed to tremble around him.

When he reached the foyer, the front door slammed shut with a force that shook the walls. He yanked it open and stumbled outside, the cold night air hitting him like a slap. He turned to look back at the manor, but the building was dark and silent, the firelight extinguished as if it had never been there.

His chest heaved as he tried to catch his breath, his mind racing. The new book felt heavier than it should have, its presence unnerving. He had the sense that he had been given a piece of the puzzle—but at what cost?

As he made his way back toward town, the shadows of the manor lingered in his mind, their secrets weaving a web that was tightening around him. He knew he was closer to the truth, but he also knew that the deeper he delved, the more dangerous the game would become.

Eight

An Invitation to Chaos

The night after his visit to the manor was one of restless dreams. The stranger awoke to the dull gray light of dawn streaming through his window, his body tense and his mind clouded by the cryptic words of the hooded man. The book he had taken from the manor lay on the table before him, its sigil glowing faintly in the dim light as though it were alive. He hadn't dared open it yet. The weight of its presence in the room was enough to keep his thoughts spinning in endless circles.

The silence of the boarding house was broken by a sharp knock at his door. He froze, his gaze darting to the book before he quickly slid it under the loose floorboard where the other artifacts were hidden. Another knock came, louder this time.

"Who is it?" he called, his voice steady but edged with suspicion.

"It's me," came the familiar voice of the auburn-haired woman.

He exhaled slowly, crossing the room to unlock the door. She stood in the hallway, her expression a mix of apprehension and urgency.

"You need to come with me," she said, her voice low.

"What's going on?" he asked, stepping aside to let her in.

She hesitated, glancing over her shoulder before entering the room. Once inside, she closed the door quietly behind her. "There's a gathering tonight. At the mayor's estate."

"And why does that matter to me?" he asked, leaning against the wall with his arms crossed.

"Because it's not just a social event," she replied, her green eyes sharp. "It's a meeting. A secret one. I overheard some of the townsfolk talking about it. They're planning something, and I think it has to do with the manor."

His brow furrowed. "Why would the mayor care about the manor?"

"That's what we need to find out," she said. "And before you ask, yes, I'm going too."

"Absolutely not," he said, his tone firm. "It's too dangerous."

She bristled at his words. "You don't get to decide that. I've already been dragged into this mess, and I'm not going to sit back while you play hero."

He sighed, rubbing a hand over his face. "Fine. But we'll need to be careful. If they're planning something at the mayor's estate, it's not going to be easy to slip in unnoticed."

"I have a plan," she said, her confidence surprising him. "The staff will be busy with the event, and the security will be focused on the main entrances. There's a side gate that leads to the garden. If we time it right, we can sneak in."

He studied her for a moment, weighing the risks. Finally, he nodded. "All right. We'll do it your way."

—-

The mayor's estate sat on the edge of town, its sprawling grounds surrounded by a wrought-iron fence topped with sharp spikes. The main gates were flanked by two guards, their lanterns casting long shadows over the cobblestone path leading to the grand house. Music drifted from within, mingling with the laughter and chatter of the town's elite.

The stranger and the woman crouched behind a cluster of bushes near the side gate, their breath visible in the cool night air. She had changed into a simple black dress, her hair tied back to avoid drawing attention. He wore his usual dark coat, the hood pulled low over his face.

"Are you sure about this?" he asked, his voice barely above a whisper.

"Positive," she replied. "The staff uses this gate to bring in supplies. It's only locked with a latch."

She reached out, her fingers fumbling with the latch until it clicked open. The gate swung inward silently, and they slipped through, keeping low as they moved toward the garden. The bushes and trees provided ample cover, but the glow of lanterns and the sound of footsteps reminded them that they were far from alone.

As they approached the rear of the house, the woman gestured for him to stop. "There's a servant's entrance on the left," she whispered. "It leads to the kitchen. From there, we can get to the study."

"Why the study?" he asked, his eyes scanning the area for any signs of movement.

"Because that's where they'll be meeting," she said. "The mayor doesn't trust anyone, not even his own staff. He'll want privacy."

They reached the entrance without incident, the door slightly ajar as she had predicted. The scent of roasting meat and freshly baked bread wafted out, mingling with the faint clink of pots and pans. Inside, the kitchen was a flurry of activity, with cooks and servants bustling about. The pair slipped past unnoticed, keeping to the shadows as they made their way down a narrow hallway.

The study was at the end of the hall, its heavy wooden door closed. The woman pressed her ear to the door, listening intently. After a moment, she nodded. "They're inside."

The stranger glanced around, his mind racing. "We can't just barge in."

"We don't need to," she said, pointing to a vent near the floor. "The grates are loose. We can hear everything from there."

He crouched down, peering through the grate. Inside the study, the mayor stood behind a large oak desk, flanked by two men in dark suits. A map was spread across the desk, and the stranger's heart skipped a beat when he recognized the sigil from the book drawn in one corner.

"This is the only way to protect our town," the mayor was saying, his voice firm. "If we don't act now, we'll lose everything."

"And what about the risks?" one of the men asked. "We're dealing with forces we don't understand."

"We don't need to understand them," the mayor replied. "We need to control them. The altar holds the key. Once we unlock its power, we'll have the leverage we need."

The stranger exchanged a glance with the woman, her face pale with shock. The mayor's words confirmed their worst fears—he was involved with the secrets of the manor, and he was willing to risk everything to exploit them.

"What if someone interferes?" the other man asked. "The stranger. The girl. They've already been seen near the manor."

"Let them try," the mayor said, his voice cold. "They won't survive what's coming."

The stranger's grip on the grate tightened, his knuckles white. He had heard enough. He gestured for the woman to follow him, and they slipped back down the hallway, their movements quick and silent.

Once they were outside, she grabbed his arm, her voice trembling. "What do we do now?"

"We stop them," he said, his tone grim. "Before they unleash something they can't control."

She nodded, her resolve hardening. "Then we need to act fast."

As they disappeared into the night, the stranger couldn't shake the feeling that they were racing against a clock that was already ticking down. The mayor's plans had set something in motion—something dark and unstoppable—and the stranger knew that chaos was waiting just beyond the horizon.

Nine

The Midnight Confession

The town of Willow Creek lay cloaked in darkness, the moon hidden behind thick clouds. Only the occasional flicker of lanterns from the houses disrupted the shadows. The stranger and the auburn-haired woman moved swiftly through the empty streets, their breaths visible in the crisp night air. Their earlier discovery at the mayor's estate weighed heavily between them, unspoken but undeniable. The mayor's plans were far more sinister than they had imagined, and the clock was ticking.

They reached the edge of the woods, the towering trees standing like sentinels in the dark. The woman paused, glancing back at the faint lights of the town. Her face was pale, her usual fire tempered by the gravity of what they faced.

"Are you sure about this?" she asked, her voice barely above a whisper.

"We don't have a choice," the stranger replied. His tone was resolute, but there was a flicker of doubt in his eyes. "If we don't act, he'll unleash something none of us can control."

She nodded, though her hands trembled slightly. "Then let's get it over with."

They plunged into the woods, their footsteps muffled by the soft carpet of moss and fallen leaves. The path ahead was barely visible, the faint glow of their lantern casting long shadows that danced and twisted like living things. The air was heavy, laden with the scent of damp earth and the faint metallic tang of the altar's lingering energy.

The stranger led the way, his movements deliberate and silent. The woman followed closely, her eyes darting nervously to the shadows around them. Every snap of a twig, every rustle of leaves, felt like a warning, as if the forest itself was trying to dissuade them.

After what felt like an eternity, they reached the clearing. The altar stood at its center, its ancient stone surface glowing faintly with the sigil that had haunted their every step. The air around it hummed with an unnatural energy, and the stranger could feel it vibrating in his bones.

He stopped a few paces from the altar, his gaze fixed on its glowing surface. The woman stepped beside him, her arms wrapped around herself as though trying to ward off the chill.

"This place… it feels alive," she murmured.

"It is," the stranger replied. He pulled the new book from his coat, its leather cover cold to the touch. "And it's waiting for something."

"For what?" she asked, her voice trembling.

He hesitated, his fingers tracing the sigil on the book's cover. "For us."

He opened the book, its pages fluttering as if caught in an invisible breeze. The symbols inside glowed faintly, their intricate designs shifting and twisting in ways that defied logic. He scanned the pages, searching for anything that might provide a clue.

The woman stepped closer, peering over his shoulder. Her eyes widened as she pointed to a passage near the center of the book. "That symbol," she said, her finger trembling as it hovered over the page. "It's the same one on the altar."

The stranger nodded, his jaw tightening. "It's a key," he said. "Or part of one."

"Part?" she echoed, her voice rising. "What does that mean?"

Before he could answer, a low growl echoed through the clearing. They froze, their eyes darting to the shadows beyond the trees. The growl came again, deeper and more menacing, sending a chill down their spines.

The stranger pulled the knife from his boot, the blade gleaming in the lantern light. "Stay close," he said, his voice low and firm.

The woman reached for a heavy branch on the ground, gripping it tightly as the growl grew louder. The shadows seemed to shift and move, coalescing into a shape that sent her heart racing. From the darkness emerged a creature unlike anything she had ever seen. Its form was a twisted amalgamation of shadow and flesh, its eyes glowing with a malevolent light. The sigil on the altar flared brightly, as if reacting to the creature's presence.

"What is that?" she whispered, her voice barely audible.

"Trouble," the stranger muttered.

The creature lunged, its movements unnaturally fast. The stranger shoved the woman aside, narrowly avoiding its attack. He slashed at it with his knife, but the blade passed through its shadowy form without resistance. The creature let out a guttural snarl, its claws raking the ground as it turned to face them.

The woman scrambled to her feet, her heart pounding. She swung the branch at the creature, but it shattered on impact, the force sending her stumbling backward.

"We can't fight it," she shouted. "What do we do?"

The stranger's mind raced as the creature advanced. His gaze flicked to the book, its pages glowing with an intensity that matched the sigil on the altar. An idea began to form, desperate and reckless, but it was their only chance.

"Keep it distracted," he said, shoving the book into her hands. "I'll handle the altar."

"What? Are you insane?" she yelled, but he was already moving.

The creature roared, lunging at him as he sprinted toward the altar. He dodged its claws, his movements quick and fluid, and reached the stone surface. The energy radiating from it was almost unbearable, but he placed his hands on the sigil and began to speak the words written in the book.

The air around them grew heavy, charged with an electric tension. The sigil pulsed brightly, its glow spreading across the altar like veins of molten gold. The creature let out a piercing shriek, its form flickering as though it were being torn apart.

The woman watched in horror and awe, clutching the book to her chest. She wanted to help, to do something, but the sheer power emanating from the altar rooted her to the spot.

The stranger's voice rose, his words sharp and commanding. The sigil on the altar blazed with a blinding light, and the creature let out one final, anguished roar before it dissolved into nothingness.

The clearing fell silent, the only sound the ragged breathing of the two figures standing near the altar. The sigil's glow faded, leaving the stone cold and lifeless once more.

The woman approached slowly, her hands trembling as she set the book on the ground. "Are you okay?" she asked, her voice soft.

He nodded, though his face was pale and drawn. "It's gone," he said. "For now."

She reached out, her fingers brushing against his arm. "What happens now?"

He looked at her, his eyes filled with a mixture of determination and regret. "We finish what we started," he said. "No matter what it takes."

The weight of his words settled over them like a shroud. The battle was far from over, and the secrets of the altar were only beginning to reveal themselves. As they left the clearing, the stranger couldn't shake the feeling that they had crossed a line, one from which there was no turning back.

Ten

A Threat in the Shadows

The forest loomed around them, an endless maze of shadows and whispers. The narrow path leading away from the altar twisted through the trees, each step muffled by the damp earth. The air was thick with tension, every sound amplified in the stillness of the night. The stranger and the woman walked side by side, their breaths visible in the cool air, their nerves frayed after the encounter at the altar.

"Do you think it's really gone?" she asked, her voice barely above a whisper.

The stranger's eyes remained fixed on the path ahead, his jaw clenched. "For now," he replied. "But that doesn't mean we're safe."

The woman shivered, wrapping her arms around herself. The

memory of the creature's glowing eyes and guttural snarls was fresh in her mind, a haunting reminder of the danger that seemed to follow them. She glanced over her shoulder, her heart racing at every rustle in the underbrush.

"We need to move faster," the stranger said, his tone sharp. "Staying here is too risky."

She nodded, quickening her pace to match his long strides. The lantern in her hand cast a faint glow on the path, the light flickering with each gust of wind. The woods felt alive, as though unseen eyes were watching their every move. The sensation was suffocating, and she struggled to keep her fear in check.

They had only gone a few hundred yards when the stranger suddenly stopped, his hand shooting out to block her path. She opened her mouth to protest, but he silenced her with a quick gesture. His head tilted slightly, his sharp eyes scanning the trees.

"What is it?" she whispered, her voice trembling.

"Something's following us," he said, his voice low. He motioned for her to extinguish the lantern. Reluctantly, she blew out the flame, plunging them into darkness.

The woman's pulse quickened as she strained to hear what he had sensed. At first, there was nothing but the soft rustle of leaves in the breeze. Then she heard it—a faint sound, almost imperceptible. Footsteps. Slow, deliberate, and unnervingly close.

The stranger drew his knife, the blade glinting faintly in the dim light of the moon filtering through the canopy. He motioned for her to stay behind him, his movements precise and silent.

"Who's there?" he called, his voice cutting through the stillness.

The footsteps stopped abruptly, the silence that followed more oppressive than the sound had been. The woman's heart pounded in her chest, her grip tightening on the lantern. She felt exposed, vulnerable, as though whatever was out there could see her clearly while she remained blind to its presence.

A low chuckle echoed from the shadows, sending a shiver down her spine. It was a sound filled with malice, a predator toying with its prey.

"Well, well," a voice drawled, smooth and taunting. "The hero and his little companion. How touching."

The stranger's stance shifted, his knife held ready. "Show yourself."

A figure stepped into the faint moonlight, his face partially obscured by a wide-brimmed hat. His dark coat blended with the shadows, and his eyes gleamed with a dangerous light. The woman recognized him immediately—Marcus, the man who had visited the stranger at the boarding house.

"Marcus," the stranger said, his voice cold. "What are you doing here?"

"Keeping an eye on you, of course," Marcus replied, his tone mocking. "You've been stirring up quite the commotion."

The woman stepped closer to the stranger, her fear giving way to anger. "You're following us?"

Marcus tilted his head, a smirk playing on his lips. "Following, watching, ensuring you don't do anything foolish. Call it what you like."

"Why?" the stranger demanded, his knife glinting. "What's your angle?"

Marcus chuckled, his hands spread in a gesture of mock innocence. "No angle, old friend. Just a friendly warning. You're playing with fire, and it's only a matter of time before you get burned."

The stranger took a step forward, his voice low and dangerous. "If you're here to warn me, then say your piece and leave."

"Oh, it's not that simple," Marcus said, his tone hardening. "You've crossed a line. The mayor isn't happy, and neither are the others. They want you gone."

"And you?" the stranger asked, his grip on the knife tightening. "What do you want?"

Marcus's smirk faded, his expression turning cold. "I want you to stop. Walk away while you still can. This town, the altar, the secrets—you don't know what you're dealing with. If you keep pushing, you'll end up like the others."

"What others?" the woman demanded, her voice shaking.

Marcus's eyes flicked to her, his smirk returning. "Didn't he tell you? He's not the first to stumble onto these mysteries. But he'll end up just like them—gone without a trace."

The stranger stepped forward, his knife raised. "Enough. If you think you can intimidate me, you're wasting your time."

Marcus laughed, the sound echoing through the woods. "Oh, I don't need to intimidate you. I just need to make you think."

Without warning, Marcus threw something to the ground. Smoke erupted around him, thick and choking, obscuring him from view. The stranger and the woman coughed, their eyes stinging as they stumbled back.

When the smoke cleared, Marcus was gone.

—-

The stranger scanned the woods, his knife still drawn. The woman clutched his arm, her eyes darting nervously to the shadows.

"Do you think he's still here?" she whispered.

"No," the stranger said, though his tone was uncertain. "But we need to move. Now."

They quickened their pace, the encounter with Marcus leaving them both on edge. The woods seemed darker than before, the shadows deeper and more menacing. Every rustle of leaves felt like a threat, every gust of wind like a whisper of danger.

By the time they reached the edge of the forest, the woman was trembling. She stopped and turned to the stranger, her voice breaking. "Who is he? What does he want?"

The stranger sheathed his knife, his expression grim. "Marcus is an opportunist. He'll do whatever it takes to protect himself and his interests. If he's warning us, it means he's afraid of what we might find."

"Or he's trying to scare us off," she said.

"Maybe both," he admitted. "But either way, we can't trust him."

She nodded, though her fear was still evident. As they stepped back into the town, she glanced over her shoulder one last time. The forest loomed behind them, dark and foreboding, as though it were watching and waiting.

The stranger led the way back to the boarding house, his mind racing. Marcus's warning echoed in his ears, a grim reminder of the stakes they faced. The secrets of Willow Creek were deeper and darker than he had imagined, and the shadows around them were closing in.

Eleven

The Price of Deception

The town of Willow Creek was shrouded in an uneasy stillness, the kind that settles when everyone knows something is wrong but no one dares to speak it aloud. The stranger stood at the window of his room in the boarding house, the morning light doing little to dispel the weight of the previous night's encounter with Marcus. His mind churned with unanswered questions, each one a thread in a web of deceit that seemed to tighten around him with every step he took.

He reached into his pocket and pulled out the fragment of metal, its etched sigil catching the light. It was cold to the touch, unnaturally so, as if it held the essence of the shadows that haunted him. He placed it on the table beside the leather-bound book from the manor and stared at the two objects as if willing them to reveal their secrets.

A knock at the door broke his focus. He slid the items into their hiding place beneath the floorboard and turned toward the door, his hand instinctively brushing against the knife at his side.

"Who is it?" he called, his voice steady.

"It's me," came the familiar voice of the auburn-haired woman. There was an edge to her tone, a mix of urgency and hesitation that put him immediately on guard.

He opened the door, and she stepped inside, her green eyes darting around the room as if checking for unseen dangers. She carried a folded piece of paper in her hand, which she held out to him without a word.

He took it, unfolding the paper to reveal a note written in the same bold, ominous script as the warning he had received days earlier.

"You've gone too far. Leave town, or pay the price."

His jaw tightened as he reread the words, his grip on the note tightening. "Where did you find this?"

"On my doorstep this morning," she said, her voice trembling. "I thought it was from Marcus, but… it doesn't feel like his style."

The stranger nodded, his thoughts racing. Marcus was a manipulator, but he thrived on direct confrontation and veiled threats. This note was different—cold, calculated, and far more dangerous.

"It's not him," he said finally, setting the note on the table. "This is someone else. Someone who doesn't want us digging any deeper."

The woman's face paled, and she sank into the chair by the window. "What do we do now? We can't just stop."

"We won't," he said firmly. "But we need to be careful. Whoever sent this knows where you live, which means they're watching us."

—-

As the day wore on, the stranger and the woman began piecing together what little information they had. The mayor's secret meetings, Marcus's cryptic warnings, the creature in the woods—every thread seemed connected to the altar and the power it contained. Yet the more they uncovered, the clearer it became that someone was working in the shadows to keep those secrets buried.

By evening, they had decided on their next move. The stranger would confront Marcus, pushing him for more information about the mayor's plans and his role in the unfolding chaos. The woman, meanwhile, would investigate the manor further, hoping to find additional clues hidden in its decaying halls.

"It's too dangerous for you to go alone," the stranger said as they prepared to leave the boarding house.

She met his gaze, her expression resolute. "I can handle myself. And if we don't split up, we'll lose precious time."

He hesitated, but her determination was unwavering. Finally, he nodded. "Be careful."

"You too," she replied before slipping out into the night.

—-

The stranger found Marcus in the dimly lit corner of the town's only tavern. He was nursing a glass of whiskey, his hat tipped low over his face. The room was nearly empty, save for a few regulars hunched over their drinks, their conversations drowned out by the low hum of a phonograph playing a scratchy tune.

The stranger slid into the seat across from Marcus without waiting for an invitation. The other man looked up, a slow smile spreading across his face.

"Well, this is unexpected," Marcus drawled, setting his glass down. "What brings you here, old friend?"

"Answers," the stranger said, his tone flat. "And I'm done playing games."

Marcus's smile widened, his eyes gleaming with amusement. "Is that so? And what makes you think I have the answers you're looking for?"

The stranger leaned forward, his voice low and dangerous. "Because you've been watching me since I got here. You know more than you're letting on."

Marcus chuckled, swirling the whiskey in his glass. "Maybe I do. But why should I share? What's in it for me?"

"Your life," the stranger said coldly. He pulled the knife from his boot and set it on the table between them, the blade catching the dim light. "Start talking."

Marcus's amusement faded, replaced by a calculating gleam in his eyes. For a moment, the two men stared at each other, the tension thick enough to cut with the very knife on the table. Finally, Marcus leaned back in his chair, his expression unreadable.

"All right," he said. "But you're not going to like what you hear."

—-

Meanwhile, the woman made her way back to the manor, her heart pounding with each step. The forest was eerily quiet, the air heavy with the same oppressive energy she had felt before. The manor loomed ahead, its shadow stretching across the clearing like a specter.

She entered through the same side door they had used before, her lantern casting flickering light on the decayed interior. The air was damp and cold, the scent of mildew thick in her nostrils. She made her way cautiously through the halls, her ears straining for any sound that might indicate she wasn't alone.

In the study where the stranger had first encountered the hooded man, she found a small chest tucked beneath a broken desk. Its lock was rusted, but she pried it open with the blade of a letter opener she had brought with her.

Inside were stacks of old papers, each covered in the same cryptic script that filled the books they had found. At the bottom of the chest lay a key, its surface etched with the same sigil as the altar. She stared at it, her pulse quickening.

Before she could examine it further, a noise behind her made her spin around. The door to the study creaked open, and a shadowed figure stepped inside.

"Looking for something?" the figure asked, their voice cold and sharp.

She backed away, clutching the key tightly in her hand. The figure stepped into the light, revealing a face she didn't recognize— a man with piercing eyes and a scar running down his cheek.

"You shouldn't be here," he said, advancing toward her. "You've meddled enough."

She gripped the key tighter, her mind racing. "Who are you? What do you want?"

The man smirked, his eyes gleaming with menace. "I'm here to ensure you don't get any closer to the truth."

As he lunged toward her, she swung the lantern, the glass shattering against his arm. Flames erupted, briefly illuminating the room as the man let out a pained yell. She seized the opportunity and bolted from the room, clutching the key as if her life depended on it.

—-

Back in the tavern, Marcus finished his tale, his expression grim. "The mayor isn't just dabbling in power—he's unlocking something ancient. Something that should have stayed buried."

"And you're helping him?" the stranger asked, his voice filled with disgust.

Marcus shook his head. "Not by choice. He has leverage. We all do what we must to survive."

The stranger stood, his knife vanishing back into his boot. "Not all of us."

As he left the tavern, his mind raced with the weight of Marcus's confession. The price of deception was steep, and as the shadows of Willow Creek closed in, the stranger realized they were running out of time to uncover the truth.

Twelve

The Town's Hidden Secrets

The next morning, Willow Creek awoke to an unnatural quiet. The usual hum of activity was subdued, and the air carried a tension that seemed to weigh on every corner of the town. The stranger and the woman met in the secluded back alley behind the sewing shop, their faces drawn and pale from the events of the previous night.

The woman clutched the key she had retrieved from the manor, its surface cold against her palm. "This was in a chest full of documents," she whispered, her voice still shaky from her narrow escape. "I don't know what it opens, but it's important. I can feel it."

The stranger studied the key, his expression grim. The intricate sigil etched into the metal was unmistakable. "It's connected to the altar," he said. "Whatever it unlocks, it's part of the mayor's plan."

"We need to act fast," she said. "That man who attacked me—he's working for someone. And whoever it is, they know we're getting close."

He nodded, slipping the key into his pocket. "Then we dig deeper."

—-

The stranger had spent the morning observing the town from the shadows, noting the subtle shifts in its atmosphere. The townsfolk moved about their day with a nervous energy, their conversations hushed and their glances wary. Something was bubbling beneath the surface, an unspoken fear that rippled through the streets like an unseen current.

By midday, he had pieced together enough information to identify his next target: the town archives. Located in the basement of the old town hall, the archives were rarely used, a forgotten repository of documents and records that held the town's history. If the mayor's plans had roots in the past, the archives might hold the answers.

The woman joined him outside the town hall, her nerves evident in the way she fidgeted with the hem of her coat. "Do you really think we'll find something here?" she asked.

"We have to," he said, his tone firm. "If the key doesn't lead us to the answers, then maybe the past will."

They slipped inside the town hall through a side entrance, their footsteps muffled by the worn carpet. The building was mostly empty, its high ceilings and dusty chandeliers giving it an air of faded grandeur. They made their way to the basement staircase, the dim lighting casting long shadows that seemed to stretch toward them like grasping hands.

The archives were a labyrinth of shelves and filing cabinets, their contents covered in a thin layer of dust. The faint scent of old paper filled the air, and the only sound was the soft rustle of their movements as they began their search.

"What exactly are we looking for?" the woman asked, scanning the labels on the cabinets.

"Anything related to the manor, the altar, or the sigil," the stranger replied. "Old records, maps, letters—anything that connects the dots."

They worked in silence, the minutes stretching into an hour as they sifted through the cluttered shelves. The woman uncovered a stack of yellowed maps, their edges brittle with age. She spread them out on a nearby table, her eyes scanning the faded lines and symbols.

"Look at this," she said, pointing to one of the maps. "The manor is marked, but it's labeled differently. 'Sanctuary of the Dawn.' What does that mean?"

The stranger moved to her side, his brow furrowing as he studied the map. The label was written in an elegant script, accompanied by a symbol that matched the one on the altar.

"It wasn't just a house," he said, his voice low. "It was a place of power. Maybe even a site of worship."

"Worship?" she echoed, her voice tinged with disbelief. "What kind of worship?"

"Not the kind you'd find in a church," he said grimly. "Something older. Darker."

—-

Their search yielded more fragments of the town's buried past: letters mentioning rituals conducted in the woods, records of disappearances that coincided with the dates of those rituals, and vague references to an enigmatic figure known only as "The Keeper."

The deeper they dug, the clearer it became that the town's history was steeped in secrets. The mayor's involvement wasn't an anomaly—it was the continuation of something that had been brewing for generations.

"This town was built on lies," the woman said, her voice trembling as she read through one of the letters. "Rituals, sacrifices, people disappearing… How could no one know?"

"People knew," the stranger said. "They just didn't want to see. Fear keeps people silent. It always has."

As they pieced together the fragments of history, a pattern began to emerge. The altar was at the center of it all, a nexus of power that had drawn people to it for centuries. The sigil was both a key and a seal, its purpose shrouded in layers of mystery and deception.

"It's all connected," the stranger said, his mind racing. "The manor, the altar, the mayor's plans—they're all part of the same web."

"But what's the endgame?" she asked, her eyes wide with fear. "What does he want?"

"Power," the stranger said simply. "Control. The altar isn't just a relic—it's a weapon. And if he unlocks it, there's no telling what will happen."

—-

As they prepared to leave the archives, a faint sound reached their ears—a soft shuffle, followed by the creak of the basement door. They froze, their breaths shallow as they listened. Footsteps echoed in the corridor, slow and deliberate.

"Someone's coming," the woman whispered.

The stranger motioned for her to stay silent, his hand reaching for the knife at his side. The footsteps grew louder, closer, until they stopped just outside the room.

The door creaked open, and a figure stepped inside. It was the man who had attacked the woman at the manor, his scarred face twisted into a sneer.

"Well, well," he said, his voice dripping with malice. "Looks like I've found the little mice."

The stranger stepped forward, his knife glinting in the dim light. "You made a mistake coming here."

The man laughed, the sound low and cruel. "The only mistake is yours, thinking you could outsmart us. The mayor knows everything. And he's already won."

The stranger lunged, his movements quick and precise. The man dodged the first strike, his own blade flashing as he countered. The room erupted into chaos as the two men clashed, their grunts and the clang of metal filling the air.

The woman grabbed a heavy book from the table and swung it at the man's head. He stumbled, momentarily disoriented, giving the stranger an opening. He drove his knife into the man's shoulder, sending him crashing to the floor.

The man glared up at them, his breathing ragged. "You can't stop it," he snarled. "The altar will be unlocked, and you'll both be nothing but dust."

The stranger's expression was cold as he pulled the man to his feet. "We'll see about that."

They left him tied up in the archives, his threats echoing in their ears as they slipped back into the night. The town's secrets were coming to light, but with every revelation, the danger grew. The altar was the key to it all, and the stranger knew that time was running out. The storm they had uncovered was building, and the price of deception was about to be paid in full.

Thirteen

The Betrayal

The air in Willow Creek was thick with an unnatural tension as the stranger and the woman made their way back to the boarding house. The events of the day weighed heavily on them, and their discovery of the town's sinister history had cast an even darker shadow over their fight against the mayor. The woman clutched the key tightly in her hand, its cold metal biting into her palm as though it carried the weight of their growing peril.

As they entered the narrow hallway of the boarding house, the stranger paused, his senses prickling. Something felt wrong. The usual creaks and groans of the old building were absent, replaced by an oppressive silence. He motioned for the woman to stay behind him, his hand brushing against the knife hidden in his coat.

"Stay alert," he whispered, his voice low and steady.

They moved cautiously toward his room, their footsteps muffled by the worn carpet. When they reached the door, he stopped again, his hand hovering over the knob. The faintest sound—a rustle, a shift in the air—came from inside. He exchanged a glance with the woman, who nodded silently, her resolve firm despite the fear in her eyes.

With a swift motion, he pushed the door open and stepped inside, his knife at the ready. The room was empty, but it had been ransacked. The table was overturned, papers and belongings scattered across the floor. The loose floorboard where he had hidden the books and the fragment was ajar, its contents gone.

The woman gasped, her hand flying to her mouth. "They've been here," she said, her voice shaking.

The stranger's expression hardened as he surveyed the room. Whoever had done this had known exactly what to look for. It wasn't a random break-in; it was deliberate.

"They're escalating," he said, his tone grim. "They're not just watching us anymore. They're acting."

"Do you think it was Marcus?" she asked.

The stranger shook his head. "This is beyond him. The mayor, his people—someone higher up is pulling the strings."

His eyes fell on a slip of paper lying on the bed, its edges torn as though it had been hastily ripped from a notebook. He picked it up, his jaw tightening as he read the scrawled words:

"It's over. Leave town before it's too late."

The woman's face paled as she read over his shoulder. "They know we're onto them," she said. "And they're trying to scare us."

"It's more than that," he said, his gaze dark. "They're playing for keeps now."

—-

As night fell over Willow Creek, the stranger and the woman regrouped in the sewing shop, the only place they felt might still be safe. They locked the doors and drew the curtains, their nerves frayed and their tempers short. The key sat on the counter between them, its etched sigil gleaming faintly in the flickering light of a single lantern.

"We have to find out where this key leads," the woman said, her voice firm despite the tremor beneath it. "It's the only clue we have left."

The stranger nodded, his thoughts racing. "The mayor's estate," he said after a moment. "If this key belongs to anything, it's there."

She frowned, her brow furrowing. "But we already searched

the estate. There was nothing."

"Not in the open," he replied. "If he's hiding something, it'll be somewhere we didn't look. Somewhere only he or his inner circle can access."

The woman hesitated, her fingers tracing the edge of the key. "If we go back there, we'll be risking everything. They'll be expecting us."

"I know," he said, his gaze steady. "But we're running out of options."

—-

Under the cover of darkness, they made their way to the mayor's estate. The streets were deserted, the town's usual quiet now a suffocating void. The estate loomed ahead, its grand facade bathed in the eerie glow of the moon. Guards patrolled the grounds, their lanterns casting long, wavering shadows.

The stranger and the woman crouched behind a row of hedges, studying the movements of the guards. They were more numerous than before, their routes tighter and more coordinated. The mayor wasn't taking any chances.

"We'll have to go through the garden," the stranger whispered. "It's the only way to avoid them."

The woman nodded, her breath steady despite the pounding of her heart. They moved silently, their steps careful as they slipped past the guards and into the overgrown garden. The scent of damp earth and wilting flowers filled the air, mingling with the faint rustle of leaves in the breeze.

As they approached the rear entrance of the estate, the stranger stopped abruptly. A figure stood near the door, their back to them. At first glance, it appeared to be another guard, but something about their stance was off—too rigid, too tense.

"Stay here," he whispered to the woman, his hand tightening around his knife.

He crept closer, his movements silent. When he was within striking distance, he grabbed the figure and spun them around, his knife poised. The woman gasped, recognizing the face immediately.

It was Marcus.

"What are you doing here?" the stranger demanded, his voice low and dangerous.

Marcus smirked, though his eyes betrayed a flicker of unease. "I could ask you the same thing," he said. "But I think we both know the answer."

"You've been working with them," the stranger said, his grip on the knife unyielding. "You're the one who betrayed us."

"Betrayed?" Marcus echoed, his smirk widening. "Oh, you poor fool. You were doomed from the start. I've just been helping you along."

The woman stepped forward, her anger overcoming her fear. "Why, Marcus? Why would you do this?"

"Because some fights aren't worth fighting," he said, his tone cold. "You think you can take on the mayor, the forces he's unleashed? You're out of your depth. The smart thing to do is cut your losses and get out while you still can."

The stranger's jaw tightened. "And what did he promise you in return? Power? Wealth?"

Marcus's smirk faltered, his eyes narrowing. "I don't owe you an explanation," he said. "But if you think you can stop what's coming, you're a bigger fool than I thought."

Before the stranger could respond, a shout rang out from the guards. Lanterns bobbed in the distance, their light drawing closer.

"We've been spotted," the woman said, her voice urgent.

The stranger shoved Marcus aside, his knife still at the ready. "We'll deal with you later," he said, his tone icy.

Marcus laughed, the sound dark and mocking. "If you survive the night."

The stranger and the woman sprinted toward the estate, their footsteps silent on the soft grass. The guards' shouts grew louder, and the sound of pursuit echoed in their ears. But they didn't stop. They couldn't.

Because whatever lay ahead was worth risking everything. Even betrayal.

Fourteen

Unmasking the Past

The mansion loomed ahead, its grand facade barely visible under the muted glow of the moon. The shouting from the guards behind them grew louder, their heavy boots pounding against the damp earth as they closed in. The stranger and the woman darted through the overgrown garden, their breaths coming fast and shallow as adrenaline coursed through their veins.

"This way!" the stranger hissed, grabbing the woman's arm and pulling her toward a hidden side entrance they had spotted on a previous visit. The small wooden door, partially concealed by ivy, appeared locked at first glance, but he had noticed the rusted hinges before.

With a swift motion, he kicked the door near the latch, the wood splintering under the force. It swung open with a groan, revealing a dark, narrow hallway. They slipped inside, and he closed the door as quietly as he could, wedging a broken chair leg against it to bar any immediate pursuit.

The air inside was stale, thick with the scent of mildew and dust. The faint hum of voices echoed somewhere in the distance, barely discernible over the pounding of their hearts. The woman leaned against the wall, her chest heaving as she tried to catch her breath.

"Do you think they saw us come in?" she asked, her voice barely above a whisper.

"Maybe," the stranger replied, his tone grim. "But they'll check everywhere eventually. We need to move."

The narrow hallway led them deeper into the mansion's hidden recesses. Faint light seeped through cracks in the walls, casting strange shadows that danced as they passed. The stranger's senses were on high alert, every creak of the floorboards and distant echo putting him on edge.

They reached an intersection of corridors, each one plunging into darkness. The stranger paused, glancing at the woman. "Do you have the key?"

She nodded, pulling it from her pocket. The metal felt cool and heavy in her hand, the intricate sigil etched into its surface catching the faint light. "Do you think it'll fit something down here?"

"It has to," he said, his voice resolute. "The mayor wouldn't hide it anywhere obvious. It's bound to be somewhere only he or his closest allies would dare to go."

They chose the corridor to their left, its uneven stone walls suggesting it led to an older part of the mansion. As they walked, the woman noticed faint markings scratched into the walls—symbols similar to those in the books they had found. The sight sent a chill down her spine.

"This place feels… wrong," she murmured.

"It's not just a mansion," the stranger said. "It's a vault. A labyrinth built to keep secrets."

They pressed on, the air growing colder with every step. The corridor finally opened into a small chamber, its walls lined with shelves filled with ancient tomes and artifacts. At the center of the room stood a pedestal, and atop it was a lockbox, its surface gleaming faintly in the dim light.

"That must be it," the woman said, stepping forward.

"Wait," the stranger cautioned, holding her back. He scanned the room, his sharp eyes searching for any sign of a trap. The air was heavy with a sense of foreboding, and his instincts screamed at him to tread carefully.

He approached the pedestal slowly, his movements deliberate. The lockbox was small but ornate, its surface covered in intricate carvings that seemed to shift and shimmer under the light. A keyhole was embedded in the center, its shape matching the key they had found.

The woman handed him the key, her hands trembling. "Be careful."

He nodded, inserting the key into the lock. For a moment, nothing happened. Then, with a soft click, the lock released, and the lid of the box creaked open.

Inside was a stack of papers, their edges yellowed with age. On top was a folded piece of parchment, sealed with red wax bearing the same sigil as the altar. The stranger broke the seal and unfolded the parchment, his eyes scanning the handwritten text.

"What does it say?" the woman asked, stepping closer.

His voice was low and tense as he read aloud. "'The altar is the key, but it is also the gate. Those who seek its power must tread carefully, for the cost is steep, and the shadows it awakens cannot be controlled.'"

The woman's face paled. "A gate? To what?"

"Something they've been trying to unlock for centuries," he said, his tone grim. He flipped through the rest of the papers, finding maps, diagrams of the altar, and records of rituals performed over the years. The final page was a list of names, each one crossed out.

"Look at this," he said, showing her the list. "These people—they were involved in the rituals. Every one of them."

She scanned the names, her breath catching when she saw one she recognized. "My father's name is here," she whispered, her voice trembling. "He… he was part of this?"

The stranger placed a hand on her shoulder. "It doesn't mean he agreed with it. Maybe he tried to stop it."

Tears welled in her eyes as she shook her head. "Then why didn't he tell me? Why didn't he warn me?"

Before he could respond, the sound of approaching footsteps echoed through the corridor. The stranger's head snapped toward the doorway, his body tensing.

"They've found us," he said, his voice low. "We need to go. Now."

He stuffed the papers into his coat, slamming the lockbox shut. They slipped out of the chamber and back into the corridor, moving quickly but quietly. The footsteps grew louder, the flicker of torchlight casting long shadows ahead of them.

"This way," the stranger whispered, leading her down a side passage. The walls closed in around them, the narrow space forcing them to move single file. The air was damp and stale, and the faint sound of water dripping echoed through the passage.

They emerged into another room, this one dominated by a

massive stone door carved with the sigil of the altar. The door pulsed faintly, as though alive, and the air around it was charged with an energy that made their skin crawl.

"This is it," the stranger said, his voice filled with awe and dread. "The gate."

The woman stared at the door, her fear warring with a strange sense of fascination. "What's behind it?"

"Something they shouldn't have tried to control," he said. "Something they still don't understand."

The sound of voices and footsteps grew louder, closing in on them. The stranger turned to the woman, his expression grim. "We can't let them get this door open."

"How do we stop them?" she asked, her voice shaking.

"We destroy it," he said, pulling a small vial from his coat. The liquid inside glowed faintly, its contents volatile and dangerous.

"You had that the whole time?" she asked, incredulous.

"Always be prepared," he said with a faint smirk.

He placed the vial at the base of the door, his hands steady despite the chaos closing in around them. "Once this goes off, the door—and everything behind it—will be sealed for good."

The woman hesitated, her gaze shifting between him and the

door. "Are you sure this is the only way?"

He nodded. "It's the only way to stop them."

The sound of approaching guards grew deafening, their voices echoing in the narrow corridor. The stranger lit the fuse on the vial, the spark hissing as it raced toward the explosive.

"Run!" he shouted, grabbing her hand and pulling her back the way they had come.

The explosion rocked the passage, the force of it throwing them to the ground. Dust and debris filled the air, and the roar of collapsing stone echoed through the mansion. When the dust settled, the door was gone—sealed forever behind a wall of rubble.

The stranger and the woman exchanged a look, their faces streaked with dirt and sweat. They had stopped the mayor's plans for now, but they both knew the battle was far from over.

The past had been unmasked, but the shadows it had awakened were only beginning to stir.

Allies and Enemies

The smoke from the explosion lingered in the air as the stranger and the woman stumbled through the hidden corridors of the mayor's mansion. Their breaths were ragged, their faces smudged with soot, but the adrenaline coursing through their veins kept them moving. The deafening roar of the collapsed passage still echoed in their ears, a constant reminder of how close they had come to being caught—or worse.

As they rounded a corner, the woman grabbed the stranger's arm, forcing him to stop. "We need to slow down," she gasped, her chest heaving. "I can't keep this pace."

He nodded reluctantly, his eyes scanning the dimly lit hall for any sign of pursuit. "We can rest for a minute," he said, his voice low. "But we can't stay here long. They'll regroup."

She leaned against the wall, clutching her side. "Do you think the explosion bought us enough time?"

"It bought us time," he said grimly. "But not enough to feel safe."

The faint murmur of voices echoed from somewhere deeper in the mansion. The stranger tensed, his hand instinctively moving to the knife at his belt. "They're close."

The woman straightened, the fear in her eyes replaced by determination. "Then let's keep moving."

—-

They slipped through the winding passages, the mansion's oppressive atmosphere growing heavier with each step. The air seemed charged with tension, as though the very walls were watching them. Every creak of the floorboards, every flicker of shadow, felt like a harbinger of doom.

At last, they emerged into a small, dusty library. Rows of ancient books lined the shelves, their leather bindings cracked and worn. A single oil lamp sat on a desk near the center of the room, its flickering light casting eerie shadows across the space.

The stranger approached the desk cautiously, his sharp eyes scanning for traps. A stack of papers lay beside the lamp, their edges curling with age. He picked one up, his brow furrowing as he scanned the text.

"What is it?" the woman asked, stepping closer.

"Correspondence," he said, his voice low. "Letters between the mayor and someone called 'The Keeper.'"

"The Keeper?" she echoed. "That name was in the records we found."

He nodded, his jaw tightening. "Whoever this Keeper is, they're the one pulling the strings. These letters talk about the altar, the gate, and… sacrifices."

The woman's stomach turned, her mind flashing to the list of names they had found in the archives. "Do they say anything about what the sacrifices were for?"

The stranger's expression darkened as he read further. "To open the gate," he said. "But not just to open it. To awaken something on the other side."

She shivered, wrapping her arms around herself. "Something… alive?"

"Alive, or something worse," he said. "The letters are vague, but they all point to one thing: power. The mayor and this Keeper are obsessed with controlling whatever is behind that gate."

Before they could delve deeper into the papers, the faint sound of footsteps reached their ears. The stranger snuffed out the lamp, plunging the room into darkness. He motioned for the woman to hide behind a nearby shelf, while he crouched low near the desk, his knife at the ready.

The footsteps grew louder, accompanied by the soft murmur of voices. Two figures entered the library, their lanterns casting long, flickering shadows across the room. The stranger recognized one of them immediately—Marcus.

"You're sure they came this way?" Marcus asked, his voice sharp.

The other figure, a wiry man with a scar across his cheek, nodded. "The guards spotted them heading toward the north wing. They can't have gone far."

Marcus's gaze swept the room, his sharp eyes narrowing as he took in the disarray. "They've been here," he muttered, his tone laced with irritation. "They're always one step ahead."

"Maybe they've already found what they were looking for," the other man suggested.

Marcus shook his head. "No. If they had, they'd be long gone by now."

The stranger held his breath, his grip on the knife tightening as Marcus's gaze lingered on the desk. He could feel the tension in the air, the sense that discovery was imminent. But then, Marcus turned away, his frustration evident.

"Keep searching," he ordered. "We can't let them leave this house alive."

The two men exited the library, their footsteps fading into the distance. The stranger and the woman remained hidden for several long moments, their breaths shallow as they waited to be sure the coast was clear.

At last, the stranger emerged from his hiding place, motioning for the woman to follow. "We have to go," he said, his voice low. "They won't stop until they find us."

—-

The pair navigated the mansion's labyrinthine corridors, their pace quick and deliberate. As they moved, the stranger's mind raced with the implications of the letters they had found. The Keeper's influence was greater than he had anticipated, and the mayor's role was only part of a larger, more insidious plan.

They reached a grand staircase that descended into the main foyer, its marble steps gleaming faintly in the moonlight filtering through the windows. The stranger paused, his instincts warning him of danger.

"What is it?" the woman whispered.

He scanned the shadows below, his sharp eyes searching for movement. "It's too quiet," he said. "They're waiting for us."

As if on cue, a figure stepped into the foyer. It was Marcus, his smirk visible even in the dim light. Behind him, several guards emerged, their weapons glinting ominously.

"Well, isn't this a surprise," Marcus said, his tone dripping with mockery. "I was wondering how long it would take you to show yourselves."

The stranger stepped forward, placing himself between Marcus and the woman. "Let her go," he said, his voice cold. "This is between us."

Marcus chuckled, shaking his head. "Oh, I don't think so. You've both been quite the thorn in our side. And now, it's time to remove it."

The guards closed in, their footsteps echoing ominously. The stranger gripped his knife tightly, his mind calculating their odds of escape. They were outnumbered, and the foyer offered little cover. But he refused to give up.

"Run," he whispered to the woman. "I'll hold them off."

"I'm not leaving you," she said fiercely, her green eyes blazing.

Before he could argue, Marcus raised a hand, signaling the guards to stop. "Enough theatrics," he said. "Let's make a deal."

The stranger narrowed his eyes. "What kind of deal?"

Marcus's smirk widened. "You give me the letters, and I let you walk out of here alive."

The woman stepped forward, her voice shaking with anger. "You expect us to believe that?"

"Believe what you want," Marcus said with a shrug. "But without those letters, you've got nothing. And if you die here, no one will ever know the truth."

The stranger's jaw tightened as he weighed their options. Marcus's offer reeked of deception, but they were cornered, and the letters were their only leverage.

"Fine," he said at last. "We'll give you the letters. But we walk out of here untouched."

Marcus's smirk faltered for a moment, his eyes narrowing. "Deal."

The stranger reached into his coat, pulling out the stack of letters. He held them out, his gaze locked on Marcus. "Your move."

Marcus stepped forward, taking the letters with a triumphant grin. But as he turned to leave, the stranger acted. With a swift motion, he threw a smoke bomb to the ground, filling the room with a thick, choking fog.

"Run!" he shouted, grabbing the woman's hand.

They bolted up the stairs, their movements quick and silent as the guards coughed and shouted in confusion below. They didn't stop until they were clear of the mansion, the cool night air hitting them like a wave of relief.

As they disappeared into the shadows, the woman glanced at the stranger, her eyes filled with both fear and admiration. "You gave them the real letters?"

He shook his head, a faint smirk tugging at his lips. "No. Just copies."

For the first time that night, she allowed herself a small, shaky laugh. "Clever."

But as they vanished into the safety of the forest, the stranger couldn't shake the feeling that Marcus's betrayal was only the beginning—and that their enemies were far more dangerous than they had imagined.

Sixteen

The Heir's Redemption

The forest enveloped them in a cocoon of darkness, its towering trees blotting out the pale light of the moon. The stranger and the woman moved in silence, their footsteps muffled by the damp earth beneath them. The tension between them was palpable, a heavy weight born of too many close calls and unspoken truths. The copies of the mayor's letters—their only real leverage—were safely hidden in the stranger's coat, but even that did little to ease their unease.

They had put distance between themselves and the mansion, but the danger was far from over. The mayor's men would regroup quickly, and Marcus's betrayal had made one thing clear: trust was a fragile thing in Willow Creek.

"We need to stop," the woman said suddenly, her voice breaking the tense silence. She leaned against the trunk of a gnarled oak, her chest heaving as she struggled to catch her breath. "Just for a moment."

The stranger hesitated, his sharp eyes scanning the forest for any sign of pursuit. After a long moment, he nodded. "Fine. But not for long."

The woman sank to the ground, her back against the tree. Her hands trembled as she reached for the canteen at her side, the cool water doing little to calm her frayed nerves. "How long can we keep running?" she asked, her voice barely above a whisper.

"Not much longer," the stranger admitted, his tone grim. He crouched nearby, his gaze fixed on the horizon. "We need to turn this fight around. Hit them where it hurts."

She looked at him, her green eyes searching his face. "And how do we do that?"

"By taking the truth to the people," he said. "The mayor and the Keeper have kept their plans hidden for years, but if the town knew what they were really up to…"

"They'd turn against them," she finished, nodding slowly. "But how do we get them to believe us? Marcus has already painted us as criminals."

The stranger pulled one of the copied letters from his coat, holding it up. "With this. And with the right timing."

—-

By the time they reached the edge of town, the first light of dawn was creeping over the horizon. Willow Creek was still, its streets empty save for the occasional stray dog or early riser. The stranger led the woman to a secluded spot near the old mill, where they could plan their next move without fear of being overheard.

"We need to get these letters into the right hands," he said, spreading the papers out on the ground. "Someone who can rally the town. Someone they'll listen to."

The woman frowned, her brow furrowing in thought. "What about the reverend? He's respected, and he's always spoken out against the mayor's policies."

The stranger considered this, nodding slowly. "It's a risk, but it might work. If he's willing to stand with us, it could turn the tide."

"And if he's not?" she asked.

"Then we find someone else," he said firmly. "We don't stop until the truth is out."

—-

The church was a modest building, its whitewashed walls and simple steeple standing in stark contrast to the grandeur of the mayor's mansion. The stranger and the woman approached cautiously, their eyes scanning the area for any sign of trouble. The town was beginning to stir, and it wouldn't be long before word of the night's events spread.

Inside, the air was cool and quiet, the faint scent of incense lingering in the air. The reverend, a thin, gray-haired man with kind eyes, was kneeling at the altar, his lips moving silently in prayer. He looked up as they entered, his expression shifting from surprise to concern.

"Can I help you?" he asked, rising to his feet.

"We need your help," the woman said quickly, stepping forward. She held out the letters, her hands trembling. "Please. You have to read these."

The reverend hesitated, his gaze flicking to the stranger. "And who are you?"

"A friend," the stranger said, his tone measured. "We don't have much time. Just read them."

After a long moment, the reverend took the letters, his eyes scanning the pages. As he read, his expression darkened, his hands tightening around the papers. When he finished, he looked up, his face pale.

"This… this can't be true," he said, his voice shaking. "The mayor—he's been our leader for years. Why would he do this?"

"For power," the stranger said simply. "And he's willing to destroy everything to get it."

The reverend sank into a nearby pew, his shoulders slumping. "If I speak out against him, he'll come after me. My congregation. My family."

The woman placed a hand on his arm, her voice soft but firm. "If you don't, he'll come after all of us. You're the only one who can stop this."

The reverend looked at her, his eyes filled with fear and doubt. But after a long moment, he nodded. "All right. I'll help you."

—-

Word spread quickly. By midday, a crowd had gathered in the town square, their voices a low murmur of confusion and anger. The reverend stood on the steps of the church, the stranger and the woman by his side. He held the letters aloft, his voice steady as he addressed the crowd.

"These letters reveal the truth about the mayor's plans," he said, his words carrying across the square. "He has betrayed our trust, and he seeks to unleash something that could destroy us all."

The crowd erupted into murmurs, their faces a mixture of disbelief and outrage. Some looked skeptical, while others nodded in agreement.

"This is nonsense!" a voice shouted, and the crowd parted as Marcus stepped forward, flanked by several guards. His smirk was gone, replaced by a scowl of anger. "Don't listen to this drivel. They're criminals, trying to sow chaos!"

The stranger stepped forward, his gaze locked on Marcus. "You're the one who's been sowing chaos," he said. "You helped the mayor hide the truth. You betrayed this town."

Marcus laughed bitterly. "And you think they'll believe you? A drifter and a—"

"Enough!" a woman from the crowd shouted. "Let him speak!"

The reverend raised his hand, and the crowd quieted. "The letters are real," he said. "I've seen them with my own eyes. The stranger and this woman have risked everything to bring us the truth. We must stand together against the mayor."

The crowd roared in agreement, their anger now directed at Marcus and the mayor. Marcus's face twisted in fury, but he held his ground.

"You'll regret this," he snarled, backing away. "All of you."

As he disappeared into the crowd, the stranger turned to the woman, a faint smile breaking through his grim expression. "We did it."

"For now," she said, her voice tinged with both relief and worry. "But this isn't over."

"No," he agreed, his gaze shifting to the horizon. "It's just beginning."

The fight for Willow Creek's future was far from over, but for the first time, they had hope—and the truth on their side.

Seventeen

A Deal with the Devil

The square was in chaos as the crowd's fury surged like a storm, their chants against the mayor growing louder. Some shouted for justice, others demanded answers, and the simmering anger felt volatile, ready to erupt. The stranger stood beside the woman and the reverend, watching the scene unfold with a wary gaze.

"We've bought ourselves some time," he said, his voice low enough for only the woman to hear. "But it won't last. The mayor's not going to let this go."

"He'll retaliate," she replied, her green eyes scanning the crowd. "We need to be ready."

As the tension in the square swelled, a sharp whistle cut through the noise. The crowd quieted, turning toward the source of the sound. A line of guards in dark uniforms had formed at the edge of the square, their polished weapons gleaming in the afternoon sun. At their head stood the mayor himself, his imposing figure framed by the towering spire of the town hall.

"Enough!" the mayor bellowed, his voice carrying across the square. The crowd stilled, their murmurs fading into uneasy silence. He raised a hand, his expression one of calculated authority. "I understand there has been some… confusion. Allow me to clarify."

The stranger tensed as the mayor stepped forward, his sharp eyes scanning the crowd. His presence was commanding, each step deliberate, as if he were walking onto a stage rather than into a den of dissent.

"These accusations are baseless," the mayor began, his tone measured but firm. "Designed to sow division and chaos in our peaceful town. And they come from outsiders—people who have no stake in Willow Creek's future."

The stranger felt the crowd's mood begin to shift, doubt creeping into their expressions. He clenched his fists, knowing that the mayor's silver tongue was as dangerous as any weapon.

"I have served this town faithfully for years," the mayor continued, his voice ringing with conviction. "Everything I've done has been to ensure its prosperity. These so-called letters? Forgeries. Lies crafted by those who wish to tear us apart."

"That's not true!" the woman shouted, stepping forward. Her

voice was strong, cutting through the mayor's rhetoric like a blade. "You've been lying to this town for years, using its people as pawns for your own gain."

The mayor turned his gaze on her, his expression cold. "And who are you to make such accusations? A seamstress? A girl with no understanding of the burdens of leadership?"

The crowd murmured, their uncertainty deepening. The stranger knew they needed to act quickly before the mayor regained full control of the narrative.

"Show them the letters," the stranger said to the reverend, his voice urgent. "Prove that he's lying."

The reverend hesitated but stepped forward, holding the papers aloft. "These documents are real," he said, his voice steady despite the weight of the moment. "I've read them myself. They detail the mayor's plans to exploit the altar and unleash powers that could destroy us all."

The crowd's murmur grew louder, anger beginning to resurface. The mayor's face darkened, his mask of calm slipping.

"You're being deceived!" the mayor shouted, his voice rising above the din. "These letters mean nothing. They are the work of saboteurs, desperate to undermine the order we've built."

The stranger stepped forward, his eyes locking onto the mayor's. "If they mean nothing," he said, his tone sharp, "then why are you so afraid of them?"

The crowd turned to the mayor, their eyes narrowing with suspicion. The tension in the air was palpable, and for the first time, the mayor's confidence faltered.

—-

Later that evening, as the crowd dispersed under the watchful eyes of the guards, the stranger and the woman retreated to the reverend's modest home. The atmosphere was heavy with unease, the specter of the mayor's retaliation hanging over them like a storm cloud.

The reverend paced the room, his hands clasped behind his back. "We've made our move," he said. "But the mayor won't let this go unanswered. He'll try to discredit us, or worse."

"He already tried worse," the woman said, her voice bitter. "We barely escaped the mansion."

The stranger sat at the table, his sharp eyes focused on the papers spread before him. "He's desperate," he said. "That means we're close to the truth."

The woman looked at him, her expression a mixture of hope and fear. "But what if he succeeds in turning the town against us? We'll be outnumbered, hunted."

The stranger's jaw tightened. "Then we don't give him the chance."

The room fell silent as the weight of his words settled over them.

The reverend stopped pacing, turning to face the stranger. "What are you suggesting?"

"I'm suggesting we go straight to the source," the stranger said, his voice firm. "The mayor isn't the mastermind behind this. He's just a pawn. The Keeper is the one pulling the strings."

The reverend paled. "The Keeper? Do you even know who—or what—that is?"

"No," the stranger admitted. "But I intend to find out."

—-

The following night, the stranger found himself standing alone in the shadows outside the mayor's mansion. He had left the woman and the reverend behind, knowing the risks of what he was about to do. This was a gamble, one he couldn't afford to lose.

Slipping through the garden's overgrown paths, he reached the hidden side entrance they had used before. The door was still ajar, its broken latch untouched. He slipped inside, his steps silent as he navigated the darkened corridors.

He made his way to the study, where the mayor often held his secret meetings. The room was empty, but the faint scent of cigar smoke lingered in the air—a sign that someone had been here recently. He searched the desk, his fingers brushing against the cold metal of a locked drawer.

With a swift motion, he pried the drawer open. Inside was a single sheet of parchment, folded neatly. He unfolded it, his eyes scanning the text.

It was a letter, addressed to the mayor from the Keeper. The words sent a chill down his spine:

"The altar's power is nearly within our grasp. Ensure the town remains under control. Betrayal will not be tolerated. The gate must be opened, no matter the cost."

The stranger's grip on the paper tightened as he read the signature at the bottom: K.

A sound behind him made him whirl around, his knife flashing in the dim light. The mayor stood in the doorway, his expression a mixture of anger and triumph.

"You just couldn't leave well enough alone, could you?" the mayor said, his voice low and dangerous.

The stranger stepped forward, his knife poised. "You're playing with forces you can't control."

The mayor laughed, the sound cold and hollow. "And yet, here you are. Alone. Outnumbered."

The stranger smirked, his eyes gleaming with defiance. "You'd be surprised how quickly the tables can turn."

Before the mayor could respond, the stranger hurled the lamp from the desk, shattering it against the wall and plunging the room into darkness. The sound of scuffling footsteps and muffled curses followed as he slipped away, the letter clutched tightly in his hand.

The mayor's voice echoed through the mansion as the stranger disappeared into the night. "You won't stop this! No one can stop this!"

The stranger didn't look back. The stakes had never been higher, and the game was far from over. The battle for Willow Creek had entered its most dangerous phase, and the stranger knew one thing for certain: the only way to defeat the Keeper was to uncover the truth, no matter the cost.

Eighteen

The Hidden Treasure

The morning air was thick with unease as the stranger and the woman gathered in the shadow of the old mill, a secluded spot where prying eyes would not find them. The town was still stirring awake, but they knew it wouldn't be long before the mayor's men began their hunt anew. The letter the stranger had retrieved from the mayor's study lay unfolded on the wooden table before them, its cryptic contents weighing heavily on their minds.

"The altar's power is nearly within our grasp," the woman read aloud, her voice trembling. "The gate must be opened, no matter the cost. What kind of power are we dealing with?"

The stranger's jaw tightened as he leaned over the table, his sharp eyes scanning the parchment once more. "Not just power," he said. "Control. The mayor and the Keeper are using the town as a pawn in something far bigger."

The reverend, who had joined them after the letter's discovery, paced the room with his hands clasped behind his back. "We're running out of time," he said. "If they succeed in opening that gate…"

"They won't," the stranger interrupted, his voice resolute. "Not if we find the altar first."

"But how?" the woman asked, her expression a mixture of determination and fear. "We've searched everywhere. If the altar is in the manor or the forest, we would have found it by now."

The stranger's gaze drifted back to the letter, his mind racing. "They wouldn't put it somewhere obvious," he said. "It's hidden. Protected. But the letter holds the key."

He tapped the parchment, his finger tracing the faint, cryptic map sketched in the margins. "This isn't just a message," he said. "It's a guide. And it points to something buried beneath this town."

—-

Following the map wasn't easy. The path it outlined was faint, leading them through winding streets, abandoned buildings, and hidden alleys. The town itself seemed to resist them, its weathered facades and creaking doors a reminder of the secrets it had kept for generations.

Their search led them to the town's outskirts, where an overgrown cemetery stretched beneath a canopy of towering oaks. The graves were ancient, their headstones worn smooth by time and weather. At the center of the cemetery stood a mausoleum, its stone walls covered in moss and ivy. The sigil of the altar was carved into the door—a chilling confirmation that they were on the right path.

"This is it," the stranger said, his voice barely above a whisper. "The entrance."

The woman shivered, her green eyes fixed on the sigil. "It feels wrong," she murmured. "Like we shouldn't be here."

The reverend placed a comforting hand on her shoulder. "Sometimes the path to the truth is the most dangerous one," he said.

The stranger approached the door, his knife at the ready. The sigil glowed faintly as he reached out, and with a soft groan, the door creaked open, revealing a narrow staircase descending into darkness.

"Stay close," he said, his voice firm. "And don't touch anything."

They descended into the depths, the air growing colder with each step. The walls were lined with ancient carvings, their meaning long lost to time. The flickering light of their lantern illuminated fragments of the past—symbols, faces, and scenes that hinted at rituals and sacrifices carried out in the name of the altar.

The staircase ended in a cavernous chamber, its walls gleaming with veins of some unknown mineral that shimmered like liquid gold. At the center of the room stood the altar, its surface etched with the sigil and surrounded by an intricate mosaic depicting a swirling void.

The woman stepped forward, her breath catching as she took in the sight. "It's… beautiful," she said, her voice tinged with awe.

"Don't let it fool you," the stranger said, his tone sharp. "Beauty like this always comes with a price."

He approached the altar cautiously, his eyes scanning for traps. The sigil pulsed faintly, as if sensing their presence. The air around it was heavy, charged with an energy that made their skin crawl.

"What now?" the reverend asked, his voice hushed.

The stranger pulled the letter from his coat, unfolding it beside the altar. "The letter mentions a hidden treasure," he said. "Something that controls the altar's power."

He ran his hands along the edge of the altar, searching for a seam or hidden compartment. After a moment, his fingers brushed against a small indentation near the base. He pressed it, and with a soft click, a hidden panel slid open, revealing a hollow space within.

Inside was a small, ornate box, its surface covered in the same glowing sigils that adorned the altar. The stranger lifted it carefully, his movements deliberate. The box was warm to the touch, pulsing faintly with a rhythm that felt almost alive.

"This is it," he said, holding it up for the others to see. "The treasure."

"What's inside?" the woman asked, her voice a mix of curiosity and dread.

The stranger hesitated, his instincts warning him of the danger. But they had come too far to turn back now. With a deep breath, he opened the box.

Inside was a single, black crystal, its surface smooth and reflective like obsidian. It seemed to hum with an energy that resonated in the very bones of those who stood near it.

"What is that?" the reverend asked, his voice trembling.

"Power," the stranger said, his voice heavy. "Pure, unbridled power."

As he held the crystal, a vision flashed before his eyes—a swirling void, a gateway opening to a realm of darkness, and the shadowy figure of the Keeper standing at its edge. He staggered, the weight of the vision threatening to overwhelm him.

"Are you all right?" the woman asked, grabbing his arm to steady him.

He nodded, though his face was pale. "We can't let them have this," he said. "If they get their hands on it…"

"They'll open the gate," the reverend finished grimly.

—-

Their victory was short-lived. As they prepared to leave the chamber, the sound of footsteps echoed from the staircase above. The stranger cursed under his breath, drawing his knife as the reverend and the woman moved behind him.

A familiar voice called out, its tone mocking and triumphant. "Well, well. Looks like you found our little secret."

Marcus emerged from the shadows, flanked by a group of armed guards. His smirk widened as he took in the scene. "Hand it over," he said, gesturing to the crystal. "And maybe I'll let you live."

The stranger's grip tightened on the box, his sharp eyes fixed on Marcus. "You're too late."

Marcus chuckled, his confidence unwavering. "Am I? You're outnumbered, and you're trapped. Be smart for once, old friend."

The stranger stepped forward, his voice low and deadly. "Come and take it."

The room erupted into chaos as the guards charged, their

weapons gleaming in the dim light. The stranger fought with a ferocity born of desperation, his knife flashing as he defended the crystal. The woman and the reverend held their ground, using whatever they could find to fight back.

As the battle raged, the crystal's hum grew louder, its glow intensifying. The stranger could feel its power resonating in his hand, a force that threatened to consume him.

"We have to get out of here!" the woman shouted, her voice barely audible over the din.

The stranger nodded, his resolve hardening. He clutched the crystal tightly and fought his way toward the staircase, the woman and the reverend close behind. The guards pursued them relentlessly, their shouts echoing through the chamber.

They burst into the open air, the night sky a welcome sight after the oppressive darkness of the chamber. The stranger didn't stop running, the crystal's hum still vibrating in his hand.

The treasure was theirs, but the battle was far from over. With the crystal in their possession, they had become the most dangerous players in a deadly game. And the Keeper wouldn't stop until the prize was his.

Nineteen

A Legacy in Peril

The air was thick with tension as the stranger, the woman, and the reverend pushed through the dense forest that bordered Willow Creek. The faint glow of dawn was beginning to break through the treetops, but it did little to dispel the oppressive weight that had settled over them. The black crystal pulsed faintly in the stranger's hand, its hum resonating in the stillness like a heartbeat.

The woman cast a nervous glance over her shoulder, her green eyes darting to the shadows that seemed to stretch and shift behind them. "Do you think they're still following us?" she asked, her voice low.

The stranger tightened his grip on the crystal, his gaze fixed on the path ahead. "They won't stop," he said. "Not until they get this back."

The reverend, lagging slightly behind, spoke between labored breaths. "Then we must decide what to do with it. This power—it's not meant for human hands."

The stranger didn't reply immediately. His mind was racing, grappling with the enormity of their situation. The crystal wasn't just a key to the altar's power; it was a weapon, one that could tip the balance in their fight against the mayor and the Keeper. But it came with a cost—one he wasn't sure they could afford to pay.

"We need to find somewhere safe," he said finally. "Somewhere they can't reach us."

The woman shook her head, her voice trembling. "There's nowhere safe, not as long as we have that thing. It's like it's calling to them."

The stranger's jaw tightened, and he stopped abruptly, turning to face her. "Then we make a stand," he said, his tone resolute. "If they want it, they'll have to fight us for it."

—-

Their journey led them to an abandoned hunting lodge deep in the forest, its weathered wood and broken windows a testament to years of neglect. The stranger pushed the door open cautiously, his knife at the ready. The interior was dark and musty, the air thick with the scent of rotting wood and mildew.

"This will have to do," he said, stepping inside. He moved quickly, checking the rooms for any signs of danger. When he was satisfied, he turned to the woman and the reverend. "We'll rest here for a while. But we need to be ready to move if they find us."

The woman set the lantern on a rickety table, her hands shaking as she lit the wick. The soft glow illuminated the room, casting long shadows across the peeling wallpaper and cracked floorboards. She sank into a chair, her exhaustion evident.

"What's the plan?" she asked, looking at the stranger. "We can't just keep running."

He placed the crystal on the table, its dark surface gleaming in the lantern light. "We figure out how to use this," he said. "If the Keeper wants it so badly, then it must hold some kind of power. Something we can use against them."

The reverend frowned, his gaze fixed on the crystal. "And what if that power is beyond our control?" he asked. "What if it destroys us?"

The stranger met his gaze, his expression unreadable. "Then we make sure it takes them down with us."

—-

As the hours passed, the tension in the lodge grew heavier. The stranger pored over the papers and maps they had collected, searching for any clue about the crystal's purpose. The woman sat nearby, her fingers tracing the edge of the table as she watched him work. The reverend paced the room, his unease palpable.

Finally, the stranger spoke. "It's connected to the altar," he said, pointing to a diagram in one of the letters. "The crystal is the missing piece. Without it, the altar can't be activated."

The woman leaned forward, her brow furrowing. "But if we have the crystal, doesn't that mean we hold all the power?"

The stranger shook his head. "Not quite. The altar isn't just a tool—it's a gate. And once it's opened, there's no telling what will come through."

The room fell silent as the weight of his words sank in. The woman looked at the crystal, her green eyes filled with both fear and fascination. "Then why not destroy it?" she asked. "If it's the key to the altar, we could end this right now."

The reverend nodded in agreement. "She's right. If the crystal is gone, so is their power."

The stranger hesitated, his gaze fixed on the crystal. The thought had crossed his mind, but something held him back—a nagging sense that the crystal's destruction might have consequences they couldn't predict.

Before he could respond, a faint noise reached their ears—a rustle outside the lodge, barely audible over the creak of the wind. The stranger's head snapped up, his instincts kicking in.

"They've found us," he said, his voice low and urgent. He grabbed the crystal, slipping it into his coat, and motioned for the others to stay quiet.

The sound of footsteps grew louder, accompanied by the faint murmur of voices. The stranger moved to the window, peering out through the cracked glass. In the dim light of dawn, he saw a group of figures moving through the trees, their dark shapes blending with the shadows.

"It's them," he said, his jaw tightening. "Marcus and his men."

The woman's breath caught, her fear evident. "What do we do?"

The stranger turned to her, his expression steely. "We fight."

—-

The first attack came swiftly. A rock shattered one of the lodge's windows, and the stranger barely had time to pull the woman to the floor before a volley of arrows followed. The reverend grabbed a piece of broken furniture, using it to barricade the door.

"They're trying to flush us out!" the woman shouted over the chaos.

The stranger nodded, his mind racing. "We need to hold them off long enough to make an escape."

He pulled his knife from his belt, his sharp eyes scanning the room for anything they could use as a weapon. The woman grabbed a heavy iron poker from the fireplace, her hands trembling as she gripped it.

The assault intensified, the men outside closing in. The stranger moved quickly, darting from window to window as he fought off the attackers. The woman and the reverend worked to reinforce their makeshift barricades, their fear driving them to move faster.

But it wasn't enough. The attackers breached the door, their shouts echoing through the lodge as they poured inside. The stranger met them head-on, his knife flashing in the dim light. The woman swung her poker with all her strength, the reverend wielding a broken chair leg as a weapon.

The fight was brutal and chaotic, the room filled with the sounds of clashing metal and shouted commands. The stranger fought with a ferocity born of desperation, his every move calculated and precise. But even he couldn't hold them off forever.

"Get the crystal out of here!" he shouted to the woman, his voice hoarse. "Now!"

She hesitated, her eyes wide with fear. "What about you?"

"Go!" he roared, his knife slashing through the air as he fought off another attacker. "I'll hold them off!"

The woman grabbed the crystal and fled through the back door, the reverend close behind. The stranger watched them go, a sense of relief mingling with the adrenaline that coursed through his veins.

As the attackers closed in around him, he tightened his grip on his knife, his resolve unshaken. The crystal was safe—for now. But the fight was far from over. And the legacy of Willow Creek hung in the balance.

Twenty

A Choice of the Heart

The forest was eerily silent as the woman and the reverend sprinted through the trees, their breaths ragged and uneven. The black crystal pulsed in her hand, its faint hum almost lost beneath the pounding of her heart. Each step felt heavier than the last, and every shadow seemed to harbor an unseen threat.

Behind them, the sound of shouts and crashing branches echoed faintly—distant, but growing closer. The reverend stumbled, his hand catching on a low-hanging branch as he struggled to keep up. The woman grabbed his arm, pulling him upright.

"We can't stop," she said, her voice trembling but resolute. "They're right behind us."

The reverend nodded, his face pale and lined with exhaustion. "Where are we going?" he asked, his voice tight with fear.

"Anywhere but here," she replied. "We just need to keep moving."

But even as she said the words, a sense of dread settled in her chest. The stranger had stayed behind to buy them time, but she knew he couldn't hold off Marcus and his men forever. The thought of leaving him behind filled her with guilt, but she forced herself to focus on the crystal in her hand. It was the key to everything—the altar, the gate, and the battle for Willow Creek's future.

As they pressed on, the forest began to change. The trees grew taller, their twisted branches interlocking overhead to form a canopy that blocked out the light. The ground beneath their feet turned soft and marshy, and the air grew colder with each step. The woman's grip on the crystal tightened as she felt its energy intensify, its hum growing louder as if in response to their surroundings.

"We're close," she murmured, though she wasn't sure what they were close to. The crystal seemed to be guiding them, pulling them deeper into the forest's heart.

The reverend glanced around nervously, his eyes darting to the shadows that seemed to stretch and shift with every movement. "This place feels... wrong," he said.

The woman didn't respond. She couldn't shake the feeling that they were being watched, that unseen eyes were tracking their every move. Her instincts screamed at her to turn back, but the crystal's pull was impossible to ignore.

They reached a clearing at last, its center dominated by a towering stone monolith covered in the same intricate sigils that adorned the crystal. The air around the monolith seemed to vibrate, and the woman felt a strange warmth emanating from it, as if it were alive.

The reverend stopped short, his eyes wide with a mixture of awe and fear. "What is this place?" he whispered.

"The heart of it all," the woman replied, her voice barely audible. She stepped forward, the crystal in her hand glowing brighter with each step. The monolith seemed to respond, its sigils flaring to life in a cascade of golden light.

Before she could reach it, a sharp voice cut through the stillness.

"Stop right there."

She froze, her breath catching in her throat. From the shadows stepped Marcus, his smirk cruel and triumphant. Behind him, his men fanned out, their weapons glinting in the eerie light of the monolith.

"You've led us right to it," Marcus said, his tone mocking. "How thoughtful."

The woman stepped back, her mind racing. She glanced at

the reverend, who was clutching a branch as if it were a weapon. He met her gaze, his expression grim.

"You won't get it," she said, her voice steady despite the fear coursing through her veins.

Marcus laughed, the sound cold and hollow. "Oh, I think we will," he said. "You can't stop us. And your friend back at the lodge? He's already finished."

Her heart clenched at his words, but she refused to let him see her fear. "You don't understand what you're dealing with," she said. "The crystal—it's not just power. It's destruction. You'll destroy everything if you open that gate."

"Spare me the sermon," Marcus sneered. "The altar's power will make us unstoppable. You think you're protecting this town, but all you're doing is delaying the inevitable."

The woman tightened her grip on the crystal, her mind racing. She knew she couldn't take on Marcus and his men alone. The odds were impossible. But she also knew she couldn't let them have the crystal—not when so much was at stake.

"Give it to me," Marcus demanded, holding out his hand. "And maybe I'll let you walk away."

She looked at him, her eyes blazing with defiance. "No."

Before Marcus could react, a flash of movement caught her eye. The stranger burst into the clearing, his knife flashing in the dim light as he dispatched one of Marcus's men with brutal efficiency. His arrival threw the group into chaos, and the woman felt a surge of relief that was quickly tempered by the realization that they were still outnumbered.

"Run!" the stranger shouted to her. "I'll hold them off!"

"No!" she shouted back. "Not again!"

Marcus, recovering from his shock, barked orders to his men. "Kill him! And get that crystal!"

The clearing erupted into violence, the stranger fighting with a ferocity born of desperation. The woman clutched the crystal tightly, her mind racing. She could feel its power, its potential, but she didn't know how to wield it.

As the battle raged around her, she realized she had a choice to make. She could run, take the crystal far away and hope to keep it out of the Keeper's hands. Or she could use it—risk everything to unlock its power and turn it against their enemies.

The reverend grabbed her arm, his voice urgent. "We need to go! Now!"

But she shook her head, her resolve hardening. "No. It's time to end this."

She stepped forward, holding the crystal aloft. Its glow intensified, the hum growing into a deafening roar. The sigils on the monolith flared to life, and the ground beneath their feet trembled.

"What are you doing?" Marcus shouted, his eyes wide with panic.

The woman didn't answer. She focused all her will on the crystal, channeling its energy toward the monolith. A beam of golden light shot from the crystal, striking the monolith and enveloping the clearing in a blinding glow.

The stranger shielded his eyes, his voice barely audible over the roar. "What have you done?"

The light consumed everything, and for a moment, it felt as though time itself had stopped. When the glow faded, the clearing was empty save for the woman, the stranger, and the reverend. Marcus and his men were gone—vanished without a trace.

The woman collapsed to her knees, the crystal falling from her hand. Its glow had faded, and it now lay lifeless on the ground. She looked up at the stranger, her eyes filled with tears.

"I had to," she whispered. "It was the only way."

He knelt beside her, his expression softening. "You did what you had to do."

The reverend approached, his face pale but resolute. "It's over," he said. "For now."

The woman nodded, her exhaustion evident. The crystal's power was spent, but the cost of their victory weighed heavily on them all. The fight for Willow Creek was far from over, but for the first time, they felt a glimmer of hope. Together, they had made a choice—not just to fight for the town, but for each other. And in that choice, they had found a strength they hadn't known they possessed.

* 9 7 8 0 7 5 5 6 7 9 0 2 7 *